by Anne E. Neimark

Latin America's Legendary Guerilla Leader

J. B. Lippincott • New York

Library of Congress Cataloging-in-Publication Data
Neimark, Anne E.
  Ché! : Latin America's legendary guerilla leader / by Anne E.
Neimark.
     p.   cm.
  Bibliography: p.
  Summary: Traces the life of the Latin American revolutionary and
guerilla fighter, from his days as a student to his death in Bolivia.
  ISBN 0-397-32308-5 : $.
  ISBN 0-397-32309-3 (lib. bdg.) : $
  1. Guevara, Ernesto, 1928–1967—Juvenile literature.
2. Guerillas—Latin America—Biography—Juvenile literature.
[1. Guevara, Ernesto, 1928–1967. 2. Guerillas—Latin America.]
F2849.22.G85N44 1989   88–23137
980'.035'0924—dc19   CIP
[B]   AC
[92]

Poem on p.vii
excerpted with permission of
Charles Scribner's Sons,
an imprint of Macmillan Publishing Co.,
from *Poems* by Alan Seeger.
Copyright 1916 by Charles Scribner's Sons,
renewed 1944 by Elsie Adams Seeger.

Maps on pages 46 and 84 are adapted from a
variety of sources by Eric Elias. Every effort has
been made to locate the copyright holders of all
copyrighted material and to secure the necessary
permissions from them. In the event of any
questions arising as to the use of these materials, the
publisher will be glad to make necessary changes in
future printings and editions.

*To my friend Susan Venus
—who always sees the whole story*

I have a rendezvous with death . . .
On some scarred slope of battered hill.

And I to my pledged word am true,
I shall not fail that rendezvous.
                              —Alan Seeger

CHÉ!

Latin America's Legendary Guerilla Leader

1

That spring day, 1939, he was eleven years old. In the courtyard of the school in Córdoba, Argentina, he crouched on the ground, drenched with water. Six of his schoolmates had dragged him under a gushing faucet. Ernesto's chest heaved unevenly, like the play of a rusty accordion. Sounds burst from his throat—the telltale wheeze and rattle of an asthmatic child. "Shove his head in water," one of the boys hooted, "and all of Argentina thunders in his throat!"

Pushing himself up, Ernesto gasped. Always the asthma was the same: the dark fire devouring spaces inside him, leaving a thickness that spit back the air. Yet he was stronger now; he'd been lifting the weights his father had bought him. Even while wheezing, he'd learned rugby and soccer on Córdoba's streets. Couldn't he fight his tormentors?

Shaking off drops of water, Ernesto leaped headlong into the heap of boys. He barely heard the shouts of Señora Rosas, his teacher, or felt her hand yanking his collar. He must change clothes! Señora Rosas shrieked. He would find pants and shirts in the health-office closet. He must hurry. He might become ill. As for the other boys, they would sit in the health office until the headmaster summoned them. They would be punished; they might be expelled.

Ernesto shut himself in the narrow health-office closet. Leaving his wet clothes lumped on the floor, he pulled on a shirt and a pair of corduroys that had been hanging on a hook. His breathing was still ragged; he hoped the boys outside the door couldn't hear it. Rubbing a fist over his chest, he imagined for one magical moment that he might tame the asthma-monster within.

The asthma had come, according to Ernesto's parents, before his second birthday. The family had been living in Rosario, in northeastern Argentina. Ernesto's father, Ernesto Guevara Lynch, had grown bored studying architecture and was milling mate, a plant cultivated for tea. On a windy afternoon Ernesto's mother had taken him to the beach, wrapping him in a blanket on the sand while she went swimming. High waves, his father later accused his mother, must have hidden Celia de la Serna de Guevara from her son's dark-eyed gaze. Surely Ernesto would have been frightened. Chilled, he'd begun coughing.

Now, in the closet, Ernesto defiantly flung his brown hair off his forehead. Was his mother to blame for the asthma? She never scolded him as she did his four younger

2

sisters and brothers. She let him ride his grimy bicycle through the parlor of the house. When asthma kept him from school, making phlegm knot in his throat, she plied him with medicines and mate, talking to him by the hour of "grown-up matters"—politics and philosophy, history and economics. Sometimes his father consoled his mother with softened words. One chill, said his father, couldn't have caused Ernesto's asthma. Didn't the finest doctors agree? The boy had a weakness. Sooner or later asthma would have attacked him.

Ernesto opened the closet door and faced his classmates lounging at the opposite wall. Coughing purposely at them, mocking his own affliction, he moved toward them. His heart pounded, but he would not let the boys see him envy their easy claim on the day's air. How he longed to prove to them that he was brave! Even if they soaked his head in an ocean of water, he would not let himself weaken enough to cry.

At a table the morning sunlight haloed a glass inkwell and two boxes of chalk and pencils. He remembered the health lecture given in assembly the week before. Students were asked not to chew on pencils or erasers. They were warned never to drink ink or to eat chalk because of the threat of poisoning. Cupping the small inkwell in his left hand, he picked up a piece of chalk from the box. Nonchalantly he thrust the chalk stick halfway into his mouth. "Join me for lunch?" he asked the boys.

"I dare you, little wheeze-boy," his classmate Miguel goaded him.

At that moment Ernesto knew he would not retreat.

3

Maybe it was crazy—maybe too dangerous—but he had made up his mind. Biting down on the chalk, he carefully chewed it into gritty pieces. Smacking his lips, he swallowed loudly. Then, saluting his former tormentors, he lifted the top of the inkwell and poured a stream of the glossy, blue-black liquid down his throat.

"Hey!" Miguel yelled. "Don't do *that*! It's poison, Ernesto! Come on, we only kid around with you."

"I'm not afraid," Ernesto said. His heart pounded so hard, it rocked his body. "Why should I be afraid of anything? I'm stronger than you think—stronger than poison."

He took another bite of chalk, his mouth prickling with the strangely sweet taste. Nearly gagging, he sipped up more swallows of ink. The oily slickness on his tongue carried off tiny bits of the chalk. Now he was remembering the white stones in Córdoba's plaza, rainwater sweeping them past the statue of the brave army hero into an open-mouthed drain.

The six other boys, unexpectedly fearful, squirmed and shuffled their shoes on the floor. They would be blamed, they knew, if they ran from the office, abandoning Ernesto to his agony. But if they stayed, wouldn't Señora Rosas say they'd forced poisons down his throat? Dazed, they leaned on each other, immobilized in the half circle they'd formed around eleven-year-old Ernesto.

The inkwell was almost empty. Deliberately Ernesto licked the edges of his lips. He would not get sick or die, he decided, from what gurgled in his stomach. The health lecture had probably been made extra scary so that Señora

4

Rosas could keep order at school. But even if he threw up or wheezed louder than ever—even if the ink crept into his veins and turned his blood black and rotten—he didn't care. How could he care, when the six boys who'd laughed at him gaped at him now with such awe? Not one of them would have dared swallow ink. Not one of them would have bitten off slices of chalk and let them dissolve in his stomach.

Sliding the inkwell across the table, Ernesto circled past the boys to the hallway door. "Don't worry so much about dying," he said, hoisting up the corduroy pants that hung too loosely on him. "I might think of war and death every day, but I'm not as afraid as you are."

He stopped, then, in the doorway before leaving the boys to await their summons from the headmaster. "Off in the Argentine jungles," he said, "there's a wild fruit, the *malanga*. It's more poisonous than ink. If I'm ever in the jungle, I'd eat every piece of a mammoth *malanga*."

Doctors in Rosario had suggested a dryer climate for Ernesto, and the Guevaras moved to the hillside town of Alta Gracia, a twenty-five-mile bus ride to school. Ernesto's father had not prospered milling mate; the only house he could afford on one of Alta Gracia's "good" streets needed repair. But the family settled into the two-story frame house on Calle Chile. Ernesto Guevara Lynch went into the construction business; his wife unpacked her political books onto tables, shelves, floors, cabinets, and chairs.

Ernesto felt a breach between his parents. Although his

5

father and mother traced their lineage to highborn Spanish and Irish ancestors, old family money was gone, seized during Argentina's long history of political chaos. Money had become as much a source of argument in the house as was Ernesto's asthma. While Celia fussed over her eldest son, Ernesto Guevara Lynch, in spite of his own business failures, pushed him to hike, run, bicycle, lift weights. "He can't *breathe*!" Ernesto's mother would shout at his father. "You'll kill him!"

"Weakness can be mastered," Ernesto Sr. would reply. "Isn't that what you've learned, Celia, in all your liberal causes?"

Liberalism—the sacred household word. Splintering any silences between the parents was Celia's embrace of the creed of the powerless rising to claim their own voice. Instead of nighttime fairy tales she spouted political philosophy. In bed at night, his door left ajar in case he choked—didn't the choking always stop his parents' arguments?—Ernesto could hear his mother's stories of endangered freedom. Heroes were praised for righting wrongs: Simón Bolívar, Pancho Villa, Emiliano Zapata, José Martí. In a bedroom mirror Ernesto gazed at his own reflection. Ribs protruded like bent arrows, legs trembled like saplings. He dreamed of freeing Argentina of corruption as Bolívar had freed Latin America from Spain. Barbells and hand grips filled his room, while an adrenaline inhaler for asthma lodged in his pocket. Grabbing a hand grip, he would squeeze downward, straining.

Sometimes the house on Calle Chile teemed with children besides Ernesto and his sisters and brothers. On the

6

next street two-story houses gave way to delapidated shacks and crumbling bungalows. Alta Gracia's poor, pressed into shabby dwellings, were ignored by wealthier families. Celia, however, invited the "shack children" into her parlor. Home from school, Ernesto might be met by a dozen dirt-smeared boys and girls. He was actually more comfortable among these children than with his own classmates. They didn't ridicule him; they stared, wide-eyed, at his barbells, hand grips, and weights. If he raced them down Calle Chile, wheezing, he could pull out his glass inhaler, spray adrenaline into his throat, and be sure the shack children still thought him tough.

After his twelfth birthday Ernesto organized a street soccer team with eleven of the shack children. The team challenged the boys who lived up the hill in palatial homes, sons of the government officials Celia condemned for dishonesty and greed. The rich boys—three of them had helped drag Ernesto under the faucet—dressed for soccer in fine cottons and wools. Ernesto wore his own "uniform" to match his teammates: stained shirt, pants held up by a rope, scuffed, peeling shoes.

Racing, dodging, and kicking down the street, Ernesto's team always scored the most goals. Excitement reigned from outdoing boys who rode polo ponies and had private servants. "Go home to your nursemaids!" Ernesto's teammates would shout in victory. Jubilantly they'd lift Ernesto onto their shoulders, their noise drowning out the hiss of his breathing. Astride them, he felt whole.

Some afternoons he wandered among the shacks themselves. It was his first real view of poverty. Flies and

7

maggots followed him; dark corners reeked of rotting food. Under a tree he'd see a baby or two wailing from inside a cardboard box. Quico, a boy stunted in growth, without eyebrows or eyelashes, usually dangled from a huge boulder. For a piece of candy Quico would agree to stick out his tongue—an ulcer-covered, yellow glob that flitted away like the flies.

Behind two of the shacks a wide hole had been bulldozed into the earth. Here lived the man with no legs. Strapped to a wheeled cart, the man was pulled from his hole by three flea-bitten, harnessed dogs, stationing himself at a town church to beg for coins or food. In rainstorms the dogs brought him back on the slatted cart like a piece of damp, rancid meat.

One Monday Ernesto was playing ball with the shack boys on a dirt patch stretched lengthwise from the man's hole. Suddenly the sound of menacing growls interrupted the game. At the rim of the hole the dogs wildly pawed their way upward. The cart appeared in their wake, bumping and scraping over the clay-mottled ground. The man's head bobbed on his neck; straps attaching him to the cart squeezed into his chest and the stumps of his thighs. Snickering, dropping to their knees as if they, too, moved about on stumps, the shack boys scooped up handfuls of stones and hurled them at the man. Only Ernesto stood aside. "Stop!" he yelled, seeing himself under the gush of the school faucet. "Leave him alone!"

Abashed, the boys rose, grinning awkwardly at Ernesto. From the nearby boulder Quico stuck out his yellow tongue. The man with no legs reined in his dogs and

8

scowled. Stones dribbled out from the creases of his arms and from the stumps of his lost legs. Ernesto stepped forward in a brief gesture of sympathy, only to see the man with no legs twist angrily toward him. Neither gratitude nor friendship gleamed in the man's eyes. Instead, mumbling in rage, he curled his upper lip and spit a stream of tobacco-laden saliva into Ernesto's face. "Get out!" he said. "Go away. *You don't belong here.*"

Ernesto slowly wiped off the spit. He did not utter a single word. The dogs, given a guttural command by their owner, hurtled forward, propelling a cloud of dust into Ernesto's mouth, grainy as the chalk he'd swallowed at school. Dust, chalk, water, ink—all paled to him in comparison to the blood of heroes. With a wheeze clogging his chest, he dreamed once more of bravery, of battling injustice. What could he have done? What might he have said? Was there a way to have convinced the man with no legs that he, Ernesto Guevara, *did* truly belong?

2

Beyond the allergy-laboratory window the darkness dropped slowly. Ernesto shifted his table lamp over a filled test tube in a rack. Dipping a syringe into the tube, he retracted the plunger until an ounce of liquid was sucked upward. His left shirtsleeve was rolled across his elbow; the skin above his wrist had been wiped clean with alcohol.

The laboratory was walking distance from the University of Buenos Aires, where Ernesto was a second-year student. He had entered the medical college, surprising his father. "I'd hoped, Ernesto," his father had said, "that you might be an engineer."

"Never," he'd answered. "I hope for much greater changes."

Personal reasons had led him to medicine. His mother,

10

living apart now from his father, had developed breast cancer. He was drawn toward the possibility of a cure through cancer research. And as always, there was his asthma. When a post had opened in the lab of pioneer allergist Salvador Pisani, he'd immediately applied. How convenient to be his own guinea pig. He was quite willing to experiment on himself.

Puncturing the skin of his inner forearm with the syringe needle, he pushed on the plunger, injecting himself with a solution of pulverized cockroach. The week before, the syringe had contained a leaf fungus and sawdust from various woods. He would determine if objects in nature triggered the allergy behind his asthma. If red welts peppered his arm or phlegm clogged his lungs, he'd have isolated at least one source of his wheezing.

Placing the syringe in a metal tray, Ernesto turned toward the window. Groups of university students were parading in the streets, brandishing burning torches. It was another political demonstration. Three years before, in 1946, when Juan Domingo Perón had become Argentina's president, students had boldly objected. They accused Perón of having secret financial ties to the United States. They claimed that greedy foreign bankers were stealing land from the local peasants. They criticized Great Britain, friend to the U.S., for keeping control of Argentina's railway.

A searing began along Ernesto's forearm. Angry blisters surrounded the needle's puncture mark, their edges fanning out like spider legs. Heat on his skin seemed to merge with the heat of the torches outside. He had carried

11

torches himself in dozens of demonstrations. Before his mother was ill, she'd taken him into crowds of *antiperonistas* marching against Perón. His arms had ached from hoisting the wooden sticks topped with flaming, kerosene-soaked rags. "Protest, Ernesto!" his mother had urged, her face tight with pleasure. "The frauds, crooks, and cannibals—they must not grow fatter!"

He braced himself now against a stricture in his chest, opening his mouth, coaxing in air. Mucus dripped in strings down the back of his throat. *Well, he must be allergic to cockroaches.* If he kept on injecting himself with bits of his allergens—bugs, plant spores, fungi, animal dander—he might be desensitized. But the process was so slow; he was so restless.

A spasm of coughing overtook him. Shoulders hunched, he tried lifting his chest out of a swamp of heaviness. He had left his inhaler at one of the part-time jobs that paid his tuition—at the night-watchman desk, or at the clerk counter at the newspaper office. He'd have to fight the asthma attack on his own. No adrenaline was nearby to relieve him, no gummy camphor to steam from the old saucepan his mother used to put beside his bed to clear his nostrils. He pressed his head against a square of window glass. The coolness distracted him from the aching in his body, but a sudden screaming in the streets jerked him upright.

Policemen, wielding guns and clubs, were herding the demonstrators into wagons. They rolled the torches in the dirt and stamped on them with their boots. Their clubs, knocked onto the heads of the more defiant students, burst through skin on forearms and ears. Ernesto caught sight of a familiar face in the semidarkness and threw open the window. His good friend Alberto was bleeding from the mouth. A policeman was yanking him over a curb and shoving him into a wagon. "Stay strong, Alberto!" Ernesto yelled through the window.

Ripping off his laboratory apron, he raced between the research tables to the door. Outside, light from a small street lamp made him squint. The wagons were moving away, sleek and silent and filled with students. Ernesto ran down the street after them. The pain in his chest did not slow him down. He had learned to hurtle past pain, leaving it behind him in some half-helpless disarray.

A mile away, at the city jail, he found the wagons parked in a row. Wheezing in hard, clattering spasms, he bolted through the jail's entrance, unrolling his shirt sleeve over the sticky welt on his left arm. He skidded to a halt at the front desk and braced himself on its wooden edge. "You have a student," he said to the uniformed clerk. "Just arrived. His name is Alberto Granados. I must see him."

The students were being processed into cells in the middle corridor. Ernesto walked quickly, a guard at his heels. The floor, cracked along its center, was scarred by the countless shoe markings of prisoners and guards. Bare light bulbs flickered from wire cages along the ceiling. In a rear cell Ernesto found Alberto propped against the metal bars. Blood had caked in his friend's hair; a purple gash sliced his cheek. "Ah, the budding Dr. Guevara," Alberto said, smiling.

Reaching through the bars, Ernesto squeezed Alberto's shoulder. To be jailed, his mother would have said, was a privilege. Hadn't some of her relatives been jailed in Spain, fighting the Civil War of 1936 on the Loyalist side? Hadn't she herself been imprisoned for yelling *antiperonista* slogans at a pro-Perón march in the Plaza San Martín? Society's evils, Celia would comment, were mankind's true cancers. Then why did he, Ernesto, stand outside the jail cell while his friend was locked inside? Was the fight in the streets worthier than his own struggles in a medical laboratory?

He kept talking to Alberto Granados until a guard insisted he leave. His fingers had clenched the jail bars as tightly as they had his old hand grips. Finally he bid his friend good-bye and retraced his steps down the scarred corridor. Out on the boulevard he passed a metal trash can stuffed with pieces of the smashed torches. He was scheduled for ten-P.M. duty at his night-watchman's job. Questions tumbled in his mind. Did he have the patience for medicine? Should he continue prying answers from test tubes while Argentina's peasants starved in hovels and were robbed of their land?

"Be a doctor if you must," Celia had said to him. "I have no time for illness—even my own. Reread Marx, Engels, and Lenin. Consider the exploited masses. Consider socialism and capitalism. Use your voice and your body, Ernesto, for the sake of the oppressed."

Over a gutter grill a stray dog lay curled in a matted heap. Had such a dog, Ernesto wondered, ever pulled a cart bearing a man with no legs? Could despair and helplessness be healed? Capitalists seemed to believe in the power of the individual, socialists in the rich filling the needs of the poor. What form of government, he asked himself, would Alta Gracia's shack children choose?

In 1951, against the advice of his teachers, twenty-three-year-old Ernesto temporarily dropped his studies. He had only one set of medical exams to complete before earning his degree, but he could not stay at the University. His restlessness hounded him. To have marched in demonstrations or to have visited Alberto in jail, to be reading more history books or to be listening to louder stories of injustice, wasn't enough. He wanted, suddenly, to immerse himself in Latin America's howling needs, to tackle suffering like an enemy. Radio broadcasts in Buenos Aires decried Nazism's twelve years of tyranny and Russia's recurring, blood-filled purges, yet Ernesto turned his attention to Central and South America. In the Dominican Republic a "people's uprising" had failed against the dictator, Rafael Trujillo. In Bolivia the election of a liberal leader, Victor Paz Estenssoro, had been overturned by the army.

Alberto Granados, released from jail, convinced Ernesto to share a motorcycle with him for a journey through Latin America. They would travel like migrant adventurers, plunging into the dark pockets of peasant misery that festered on the grand plantations of Argentina, Bolivia, Peru, and Brazil. They would, like Ernesto's childhood heroes, live closely among the ill, the starving, the illiterate, the poor.

15

Ernesto took only one change of clothing on the motorcycle trip. He left almost all his belongings at Celia's house. Once more his "uniform" included pants held up by a rope. In his knapsack, toying with the idea of keeping a journal or of writing poems and stories in the fashion of the Frenchman Baudelaire or of Chile's Pablo Neruda, he packed notebooks and pens.

Motorcycling across the great plains of Argentina's dry Pampa, alfalfa flattening under a wind, Ernesto and Alberto joined bands of gauchos at makeshift campsites. Sharing in the *carne asada*, a roasted beef, sipping mate from gourds, Ernesto savored the outdoors. But on the steep rise of the Andes mountains, Alberto's motorcycle, a secondhand purchase, began sputtering. Stones had torn the tires, and oil leaked from the tank. On the downslope, heading past the border to Santiago, Chile's capital city, the motorcycle broke down. The two adventurers had no repair money; they had to abandon their vehicle and hike or hitch rides.

Ernesto and Alberto worked at various jobs on the trip. They became stevedores on a ship, dishwashers in a restaurant, salesmen on the streets. Walking the wharves and waterfront alleys of coastline cities, they slept among *borrachos*, drunken derelicts, in rat-infested rooms. To reach Peru they crossed the arid North Chile desert of Atacama on a road built by the ancient Incas. For a week they visited backward areas near Cuzco, wandering among Quechua and Aymara Indians who'd settled in poverty across Bolivia and Peru.

In the eyes of the Indian peasants, Ernesto saw a blank-

16

ness like death. Indians labored for just a few cents a day at the mercy of pitiless landowners. Speaking in the Indian language of Quechua, Ernesto tried approaching several Indian children, but distrustful of his lighter-colored skin, they ran off.

Alberto had worked as a biochemist in an Argentine leper colony, and he and Ernesto decided to visit another leprosarium in San Pablo, Peru, on the banks of the Ucayali River, a tributary of the Amazon. It was an odyssey, Ernesto wrote in one of his notebooks, that might have interested Dr. Albert Schweitzer, the jungle doctor. An eleven-hour mule ride over dangerously steep trails took the two adventurers to a Dr. Hugo Pesche, founder of the San Pablo colony. With the doctor's letter of consent to enter the leprosarium, they were able to board a boat on the Ucayali. The humid rain forests, however, gave Ernesto severe asthma. Grudgingly he agreed to delay the journey for two bedridden days while he labored at breathing. As soon as he could stand up, he was back on the boat.

At the colony Ernesto convinced the administrators that he and his friend were licensed doctors who should be permitted to work in the medical lab where sulfone drugs were helping arrest the ravages of leprosy. Yet while Alberto pored over charts, Ernesto sat among the lepers. Men, women, and children were covered by open, pus-filled abcesses. Faces were bloated into disfigurement. Doctors at the colony wore masks and gloves, hardly touching their charges, but Ernesto refused such protection. Beckoning the lepers toward him, he played soccer

17

with them and took them hiking. In the early mornings he organized monkey hunts with the boys and girls. Unlike the Quechua and Aymara children, the leprosy-stricken young people followed him everywhere.

A seven-year-old boy, Paulo, had lost a foot to the disease. Undaunted, he hopped bravely alongside Ernesto, entranced by the dark-haired foreign man who touched him and actually held his hand. "Will I make you ill?" Paulo asked sadly when Ernesto picked him up to peer into a tree for monkeys.

"You make me feel quite well," Ernesto answered him.

In the weeks spent at San Pablo's colony Ernesto lightened the lepers' spirits and helped them laugh. Death, the leprosarium's dogged companion, dragged its feet. Yet on the evening of June 21, 1952, the two travelers prepared to leave. They stood on a bridge separating the lepers' huts from the staff quarters. In affection, the lepers had built their visitors a raft that sported a thatched roof and would carry them onward toward the Amazon town of Leticia.

Ernesto climbed onto the raft, its roof pole tied by rope to the shaky pier. A drizzle of rain pattered down on him. On the river, bobbing slowly, was a white boat crewed by the lepers. On the shore waited the colony's staff members. "Thank you!" Ernesto called toward the boat. *Never give up!* He pulled Alberto onto the raft beside him, hearing a sudden, sweet singing. The lepers, tears streaming down bloated faces, were serenading their two "doctor" friends in a heartfelt farewell. Gripping the mast of the boat was Paolo, his eyes fixed unwaveringly on Ernesto. The high-pitched tremble of the young boy's voice pierced the shadows that crept in from the hills.

18

The raft was untied, and Ernesto saw the shadows envelop Paolo's head. For a moment the boy was his own ill, childhood self, clinging to life on a mast. The lepers' songs had become plaintive now in their hush. An accompanying hymn, offered by staff members on shore, sounded its low, majestic tone.

The doctors and nurses, Ernesto would write in his notebook, and he and Alberto, and the hundreds of lepers—all were on a journey, though some might not return. But at the San Pablo pier, raft and boat moving in opposite directions, a sense of brotherhood united everyone. Waving at Paolo, Ernesto caught his breath before it stung in him. So much needed to be changed, he reminded himself. His trip with Alberto had taught him that for good. So much had to be torn away before being resurrected. Weakness and loss, he wanted to shout, tyranny and pain— these were the constant and pressing enemies.

3

The sensation of movement became a comfort to Ernesto. Pacing rooms or walking streets, switching cities or even countries, made him feel more in control. Moving about might show him which battles to join. New leaders on new missions might summon him to help in some engrossing rescue.

Returning from his trip with Alberto, he spent a frenzied six months studying to pass his medical exams. He persuaded Celia to begin cancer treatment; he wrote monographs on allergy and dermatology. But in March 1953, when he earned his degree, he had made no plans to practice medicine. He'd promised to meet Alberto in Venezuela. Repacking his knapsack, he talked a student, Carlos Ferrer, into traveling with him from Buenos Aires. They would, Ernesto said, head for Caracas, Venezuela, through Bolivia, Peru, Ecuador, and Colombia. Money would be eked out en route; momentum would keep them going.

In July, Ernesto's parents saw their eldest son off at the General Belgrano Railway Station in Buenos Aires. Neither father nor mother spoke a word to each other. Ernesto, however, waved at both of them as he and Carlos Ferrer boarded a milk train for Bolivia. "Here goes a soldier of Latin America!" he called to his mother above the screech of the train.

Ernesto's second Latin American journey drew him more deeply into politics. He had known that Bolivia was in the midst of political upheaval, the result of a recent takeover by the liberal MNR—Nationalist Revolutionary Movement—which consisted of tin miners, peasants, and army deserters. The MNR had defeated Bolivia's professional army. To improve conditions, the movement was nationalizing the mines where young workers died of lung disease; it was also splitting up the *latifundias*, the huge estates hoarded by the rich. In the spirit of Simón Bolívar, who'd proclaimed the early settling rights of Latin America's Indians, the MNR announced land reform as part of its victory. Peasants, to the horror of wealthy landowners, were being issued certificates entitling them to parcels of land.

On the sloping streets of La Paz, Bolivia's capital, Ernesto and Carlos Ferrer encountered daily gunfire between MNR fighters and uncaptured army soldiers. Exuberant parades flashed amid the shooting, extending along the outdoor Camacho market and beside bustling

21

cafés. "Are you with us, pal?" paraders would ask Ernesto, using the slang word "*che*," which meant "pal" or "buddy." "Where do you come from? Do you support the people?"

Ernesto would give an "okay" sign, but he felt critical of certain MNR reforms. The new Bolivian leaders, supposedly liberal, were creating their own tyrannies; they seemed to not truly respect the peasant. One day, grabbing Carlos by the arm, Ernesto yanked him down six blocks to the Ministry of Peasant Affairs. Indians, somber faced under frayed sombreros, waited in long lines for their land certificates. "Look up the staircase!" Ernesto said to Carlos. "What an atrocity!"

On the second floor an MNR deputy held a rubber hose that was attached to a motorized tank. As each Indian shuffled forward, the deputy thrust the hose down his back, spraying a dense cloud of powder. "Insecticide," Ernesto said, wheezing and coughing. "The MNR has decided to kill lice by treating these starving peasants like barnyard animals. Cruel leaders are defeated, Carlos— only to have new leaders turn cruel."

When Ernesto and Carlos Ferrer left Bolivia for Peru and Ecuador, they were traveling with four just-met political dissidents. In a series of border towns infested with yellow fever, one of the men, Ricardo Rojo, talked incessantly to Ernesto of Guatemala. "Forget your friend in Caracas," Rojo said. "A real revolution is happening in Guatemala. Foreign imperialism is the target. The United Fruit Company of the United States has been stripping Guatemala of its resources. Poverty is epidemic. Eight out

22

of every ten Guatemalan children wear no shoes. Seven out of ten are illiterate. *Go see Guatemala.*"

Ernesto was carrying medical instruments as well as notebooks in his knapsack. He and Alberto Granados had planned to practice jungle medicine or to visit the Venezuelan leprosarium. But he was realizing that "to be a revolutionary doctor," as he wrote home to his mother, "there must first be a revolution." In Guatemala the three-year-old government, led by a Colonel Jacobo Arbenz, was encouraging Communist support as it fought against the United Fruit Company. Opposition forces, backed by U.S. CIA agents, had been converging on the country's capital, Guatemala City. *Yes,* Ernesto answered Ricardo Rojo, Alberto Granados might understand if Ernesto changed his destination to Guatemala.

Thumbing his way northward for three weeks, Ernesto arrived alone in Guatemala City. Carlos Ferrer and the other four men remained in Peru. He located a shabby sleeping room in a Quinta Avenida pension, a boarding-house, where university students and political exiles rented space. Searching for work, he was able to hire on at a book company as a door-to-door salesman. His shoes had lost their heels, but he walked on them anyway. In the open cafés he listened to the political philosophy of the bearded exiles—Marxism, Leninism, anarchy, democracy. What, he kept wondering, was his own political voice? He read some of the books he was selling, studying a thousand-page volume on the military strategy of the Spanish Civil War.

Guatemala was a political fever to those in its cities.

23

Visiting U.S. officials, advised by their Secretary of State, John Foster Dulles, were pressuring Colonel Arbenz to establish a capitalist democracy and to reject any Communist influence. Rumors abounded that a small, U.S.-backed mercenary army was being trained in Honduras to invade Guatemala. The U.S., eager to protect the United Fruit Company, was said to be preparing an air drop of leaflets encouraging volunteers to the mercenary army.

In the pension Ernesto had met a young Peruvian exile named Hilda Gadea. Seeing how thin he was, Hilda began cooking Ernesto's meals. She learned to give him injections of adrenaline for his wheezing, but more than nurturing his health, she worked on his mind. A confirmed Marxist, outspoken in spite of Latin America's tradition of subservient women, Hilda lectured Ernesto on what she called the dangers of *imperialismo yanqui*—Yankee imperialism. She introduced him to Cuban exiles whose young, leftist political leader, Fidel Castro, had been imprisoned for sparking an attack on the Moncada Army Barracks in Cuba. The attack, Hilda told Ernesto, was a protest against the dictatorial regime of Cuba's president, Fulgencio Batista.

Hilda, black haired and of Indian ancestry, did not physically resemble Ernesto's mother, but she represented many of Celia's dogmatic biases and beliefs. Though Ernesto refused her request to join the Communist Party in Guatemala—he would, he said, form opinions as an independent—he attended political meetings with her where

24

anti-American sentiment was high and where leftist policies were developed.

In June of 1954 the rumored U.S.-backed army invaded Guatemala. No one in the cafés seemed worried. Six or seven hundred mercenaries, said the bearded exiles, had no possible chance against Guatemala's revolutionary force of seven thousand men. Yet Ernesto sensed a lack of accord between Colonel Arbenz and the military. He tried to convince student groups meeting in the pension to station themselves in the capital building where, armed and occupying a point of power, they could help defeat the invaders. From his readings of military strategy he suggested that weapons be distributed to union and peasant groups—and to political factions that had professed loyalty to the revolution.

No one besides Ernesto and Hilda seemed willing to take immediate action. Procrastination flourished, the revolutionary army making only an ineffective counterassault on the mercenary troops. "If Arbenz doesn't do something," Ernesto said to Hilda, "the United Fruit Company will keep its stranglehold on Guatemala."

On a mid-June night, several bombs exploded outside the pension. Ernesto and Hilda ran into the street, their heads and shoulders clouded by black ash from the building's seared awning. "A bomb just hit the radio station and capital headquarters!" someone screamed. "Fires are burning all over the city!"

Ernesto pulled Hilda behind an empty peddler's cart. He knew that the utterly impossible was happening—

Guatemala's soldiers were somehow failing against the mercenaries. The three-year-old Guatemalan revolution, praised by so many as a gift to the poor, was crumbling in the streets. It was already rumored that Colonel Arbenz might flee the presidency, that Guatemala's right wing, poised for the liberals' downfall, had been mapping out a bloody purge of the government.

"Who are those soldiers down the street, Ernesto?" Hilda suddenly cried out from the side of the peddler's cart.

Ernesto peered past a street lamp, ash and smoke leaving him almost breathless. He could barely identify the rifles stretched across chests or the domed rise of the helmets. Boots thudded forward over the cobblestones. Then he heard Hilda gasp. "Oh," she said, "it's the mercenaries, not our own soldiers. The United Fruit Company is winning again—rich at the expense of poor."

Two Cuban exiles from the pension scrambled behind the peddler's cart. A cold angle of metal, a gun, was slapped into Ernesto's hand. Once, he had gone pellet shooting with his father in Rosario, the crescent moon of revolver trigger tempting his finger. This gun, however, would contain real bullets. If he aimed and fired it, he could kill a human being. In return, *he* might be killed. Yet he had always refused to quake over death. That was the message he had wished he could give Guatemala's Indians: Don't be afraid. Challenge death and you shall be free.

The front guard of the mercenaries reached the corner.

26

One soldier laughed raucously and stopped to kick an old, straw-hatted peasant who sat, head bowed, on the ground. Ernesto spun the gun into position in his hand and raised it to chest level. *How else,* he asked himself, *to avenge the revolution's fall?* Gauging that a bullet would slam into the torso of the laughing soldier, he pressed the curve of the gun trigger only slightly as Hilda whispered at his side. On the next squeeze, he thought, he would invite death, even though his degree in medicine was meant to ensure life. Could death sometimes be a cure?

"Killing an intruder tonight," said a nearby voice, "will never save Guatemala's revolution."

Ernesto veered from his target to confront a painfully thin, wiry man whose eyes seemed to steam in the shadows. With a hesitant nod, he slowly lowered the gun until it pointed at the street. "Right," he said to the stranger, relieved that, for the moment, he had not needed to unleash death onto life. "Who are you?"

"Julio Valle," the man said. "Guatemalan. Tonight is only one political failure, my friend. In Guatemala, Peru, Bolivia, Cuba—wherever—the people will rise again. And you? Who are you?"

Ernesto opened his mouth to reply. *Well, then,* he thought, *who am I?* The puny, asthmatic child? The captain of the shack soccer team who'd lifted weights and clutched hand grips; a hitchhiker; a doctor? More important to him than any label was his hunger for some gesture that would permanently connect him to those who unjustly suffered. He remembered the word *"che"* tossed at

27

him by the paraders in Bolivia's Camacho market, the universal salutation of "pal" or "buddy," the name that could belong to anyone. "Me?" he answered Julio Valle— or answered himself—casting aside his old name, gulping in air as if it could be catapulted into his lungs, could help him vault over a chasm. "I'm . . . *Ché.* From Argentina. From all of Latin America. My name is Ché Guevara."

4

Click. The camera, light as a dime-store toy, snatched its mother-and-child image from the park-bench seat. Ché (Ernesto) Guevara turned a knob on the camera's side until the next snapshot number showed in a plastic window. He smiled briefly at the woman who sat on the bench with her child. "We'll deliver the pictures, Señora," he said. "You won't regret purchasing a memento of Mexico City."

Jumping toward the bench, his face tanned from the July sun, Julio Valle shook the woman's hand. "Beautiful pictures!" Julio boasted. "We take beautiful pictures!" Bowing, he tipped his cap. "Come on, Ché," he mumbled. "Let's snag other tourists."

The sound of his new name settled easily in Ché's ears. Much of Ernesto Guevara had been left among the rubble of the bombings in Guatemala. He and Julio Valle had escaped the purge of government sympathizers by hopping a train to Mexico City. Hilda had joined them in a cheap apartment at 40 Calle Napoles. She had suggested Mexico, its cities a haven for political exiles; and the self-baptized Ché now considered himself an exile. He was no longer welcome in Guatemala. He would not go home to Argentina. Instead of practicing medicine, he was searching for the revolution that could succeed. "My stethoscope and my vials of pills," he'd told Julio, "aren't weapons enough."

In Mexico, Ché and Hilda had decided to marry. They were, if not star-struck lovers, deeply close comrades. Hilda was employed as a typist in a Mexico City office; Ché had been hired as a part-time allergist at the city's General Hospital and was taking and selling photos in the parks with Julio Valle. On their off-hours, however, Ché and Hilda were together. They read aloud from Dostoyevsky's novels and from Freud's volumes on psychoanalysis. One weekend they hitchhiked into the country to visit the famous poet León Felipe. Yet, invariably, their talk turned to politics. Modern revolutionaries, they agreed, were moral failures who vowed dignity and full stomachs for the poor but who ended up placating imperialists and stabbing the poor in the back. A truly moral leader, the two said, would never surrender to insecurity or greed.

The Guevara–Gadea marriage took place in Mexico City on August 18, 1955. In mid-February 1956 Hilda gave birth to a daughter named for her mother but to be called Hildita, or "little Hilda." Leaving her job, Hilda stayed home to nurse the baby. By then the exiles in Mexico City's cafés were aflame with political queries. Would the recent Algerian insurrection against the French, they asked, rise anew? Would the Communists gain strength in Vietnam now that they'd occupied the camp Dien Bien Phu? Would Fidel Castro, released from a Cuban prison, lead a second rebellion in the name of the people against the U.S.-backed Batista regime?

Photographing tourists that July day in the park, Ché finally tucked his camera into Julio Valle's pocket for safekeeping and went to his shift at General Hospital. He'd collected blood samples from the hospital cooler and was carrying them down a corridor when he saw two men at a doorway—Cuban exiles he'd known in Guatemala. The one named Ñico raised an eyebrow, grinning, and fished a slip of paper from his jacket. Handing the paper to Ché, he pointed to a scrawled street address on Calle Emparan. "*He* is there," Ñico whispered. "*Fidel.* Fidel Castro! Pay him a visit if you still like revolution. He accepts visitors."

That evening Julio Valle volunteered to watch baby Hildita while Ché and Hilda strolled in some curiosity toward 49 Calle Emparan. Welcomed into an upstairs apartment, they were introduced to a ruddy-faced, black-bearded Fidel Castro. Over two dozen men and women were crammed into the narrow parlor. Cigar smoke made Ché wheeze, but he hid the sounds by inhaling in shallow breaths. Gesturing, Fidel led him into a steamy, lino-leum-tiled kitchen, leaving Hilda to visit in the parlor with

31

old friends. Ché was struck by the deference shown by everyone to Fidel Castro. Eyes shifted to the man's every move, voices vied for his attention. "Fidel . . . Fidel" began and ended every sentence.

What was so special, Ché wondered, about this bearded revolutionary who stirred spaghetti in a pot on the kitchen stove? When the Cuban exiles in Guatemala had raved over Fidel's bravery, Fidel's intelligence, Fidel's craftiness, Fidel's wisdom, he'd only half listened. In the smoky Mexican kitchen, however, he mulled over the stories. At age fourteen Fidel had organized a strike of sugar workers against his own plantation-wealthy father. At age twenty-six, imprisoned after the attack on the Moncada Army Barracks, he'd issued frequent communiqués. *Unite all who can be united,* he'd said, *in the cause of social justice.*

Not an hour passed before Ché Guevara and Fidel Castro were locked in conversation. "I think I have been waiting for you," Fidel said, launching into his private agenda for the future. Over the next year he planned to rent an abandoned farm outside Mexico City. A retired army officer, a Colonel Bayo, would train a group of men there as guerilla fighters—social reformers who would take up arms to aid the people against oppressors. A guerilla fighter, Fidel explained, must be willing not only to kill but to die. He must be committed to uprooting the social system that trapped all his unarmed brothers in misery and ignorance.

"And you'll do what with your guerillas?" Ché asked.

"I will put them on a boat," Fidel said. "I'll sail with them to ignite a victorious revolution in Cuba. Either we

32

will be killed or we will become free men. I've talked to you for the first time tonight, Guevara, over spaghetti—but I invite you to join me."

Amazingly, Ché's wheezing disappeared, overcome by a smothering excitement. A *victorious* revolution? he repeated to himself. Had he found, at last, the essential ingredient? Was this man, this Cuban, Fidel Castro, as powerful as he seemed? Was he the mutineer with the special cause, the leader who would not topple?

Thinking of Hilda, who waited for him, and of the baby; of Alberto Granados, working in a Venezuelan leprosarium; and of Julio Valle, exiled in Mexico, Ché knew that, whatever or whoever he'd been before, he must test out Fidel Castro's plan. The guttural Cuban voices in the crowded kitchen, the smell and tang of sweat and of future revolution, blended into a sense of something irresistible. The mission had come. Ché would soon write of his fateful spaghetti meeting with Fidel Castro: "I knew him on one of those cold nights in Mexico, and . . . within a few hours—at dawn—I had become one of his future revolutionaries."

The revolution, Fidel said, would be in behalf of Cuba's have-nots. Misused power would be wrenched from the hands of Fulgencio Batista, dictator, and returned to the people. In 1898 Cuba had gained its independence from Spain. In 1956, with only a motley crew of eighty-one guerilla fighters and limited funds, Fidel would launch his own battle for freedom.

At two A.M., November 25, 1956, Ché snuck across the

33

wharf of the Mexican gulf port Tuxpán. The Cubans who'd trained with him on the farm bunched awkwardly behind him. Boxes of machine guns, rifles, pistols, grenades, and ammunition were supported on shoulders. Rain poured so heavily that no one noticed the NO NAVIGATION sign posted by weather-wary authorities, but reading the sign would have made no difference. The men had completed their training. The boat to secretly transport them to Cuba stirred beside the wharf, and though the *Granma*'s capacity was marked at twelve to fifteen people, all eighty-two men would pile aboard. "It is time," Fidel had said. "The moment descends."

Jumping onto the boat's deck, Ché didn't bother to glance back toward Tuxpán. Families had not been told of departure; Hilda and the baby, whom he hadn't seen for weeks, would be asleep in their beds. The only announcements made by Fidel were on radio to the Cuban people, promising them that the *rebeldes*, the rebels, would rescue them. Trucks and supplies awaited the *Granma* at Niquero on Cuba's southeastern coast. A sympathetic student riot would, at the proper moment, erupt in Santiago de Cuba.

Touching the gun at his belt, Ché tilted his face to the rain. He was where he most wanted to be—snared by the struggle. No matter that it might seem crazy for Fidel to send eighty-two men in a tiny pleasure boat to confront an army of thousands. This was not Guatemala. Fidel's voice pulsed conviction. *"Human dignity,"* Fidel said, *"must be reclaimed. A sacrifice of lives would be more than worthwhile."*

34

The *Granma* slipped into the rainy darkness, shoved sideways by the wind. Two of the Cubans helped Ché tie down the weapon boxes at the railings. Though Ché was a foreigner, not a native Cuban, he was treated with respect. Fidel's Colonel Bayo had called him the "best trainee." Guevara was short, Colonel Bayo had pointed out—and he doubled over with coughing fits—but he was a gritty fighter. "A coughing *bandito*," Colonel Bayo had joked.

By morning a storm had rolled out of the western sky. The boat rocked back and forth like a pendulum, tossing hundreds of fish onto the deck. Men suddenly fell ill from seasickness, their vomit blown back in their faces in slimy, rust-colored lumps. Ché was the only doctor on board, and he dispensed medicine from his knapsack. The stench of vomit inflamed his lungs, but for once even he could not hear the wheezing. The winds roared, the men shouted, the tumultuous gulf waters smashed against the boat. "We're coming, Cuba, like the truth!" Ché yelled across the storm.

For nine days the small, teeming boat that heralded Fidel Castro's revolution heaved forward toward Cuba. On the tenth day, with land in sight, the men were shaking from weakness. Beached at a southeastern shoreline, they lugged supplies off the boat, scrambling into a prickly salt marsh, their faces stung by mosquitoes. A half dozen boxes of arms and ammunition were left behind, too heavy for sagging shoulders. Ché and Fidel peered through binoculars. "If we're anywhere near the trucks at Niquero," Fidel said, "we'll have more supplies."

The men staggered dizzily over the marshy land, staring up at the mountain peaks of the Sierra Maestra. Their training from Colonel Bayo had been on much drier soil. In the salt marshes mud oozed over their shoes and sucked at their feet, slowing their pace. Several men stopped to rest or drink from canteens, but Fidel urged them onward. Ché threw his own canteen to a man who still vomited. "Drink!" Ché said, his voice a sharp rasp. "The revolution needs you!"

At nightfall Ché realized that what the *rebeldes* needed was a good night's sleep. Fidel was tramping across a sugarcane field, but reluctantly he gave the signal. The men lowered their heavy boxes, dropped their knapsacks, loosened their belts. Rations were passed among them. They stretched out under floppy cane leaves, ate, grumbled, exchanged details of guerilla tactics, and fell asleep. Exhaustion kept them sleeping so deeply that it was Ché who awoke before dawn to an ominous drone of overhead buzzing. He lay on his stomach, moist dirt having stained his rumpled uniform. Rolling to one side, he momentarily forgot his whereabouts, but something made him listen to the grating, persistent noise.

An army airplane . . . three or four! Leaping to his feet, Ché roused the man next to him, shouting to the rest. The *rebeldes* had been discovered. News of their impending landing must have put Batista's troops on alert across the island.

The half-drowsy men tried to scatter over the field to avoid the strafing of aircraft fire. Ground soldiers poured

36

suddenly from a ring of woods, the paths of bullets both horizontal and vertical. Shattering sound seemed to bend the cane leaves in a synchronized rhythm. Within twelve minutes the planes had flown off, the soldiers surveyed their handiwork, and only fifteen out of Fidel Castro's eighty-two guerilla fighters had escaped by clawing their way across the field onto tree-covered lower ridges of the Sierra Maestra.

The survivors hid singly or in pairs until the onslaught was hours old and the soldiers had withdrawn. Then the remaining *rebeldes* counted each other and sought each other out. Faces were grim; words were spare. Kneeling beside a flat-topped boulder, Ché was grateful to see that Fidel and his brother, Raúl Castro, were safe. Another Cuban, Urbano, joined Ché at the boulder. "We're finished," Urbano said bitterly, "before we've even begun. Sixty-seven of us dead before sunrise."

"Fifteen of us alive," Ché answered at once.

Urbano, eyes flashing, shook his head in disgust.

"Fifteen?" he said. "*Fifteen?* We were insane enough, Guevara, to buy the scheme of eighty-two guerillas starting a revolution. Batista's army must be everywhere. What medicine in your knapsack is strong enough to make a revolution with fifteen men?"

Ché tapped his chest. "Heart," he said flatly, "not medicine. Heart, Urbano—and the favors we'll steal from Fate."

Pulling the Cuban to his feet, Ché returned a beckoning wave from Fidel. "Move, Urbano!" Ché said, prodding his fellow guerilla across a tangle of shrub needles. "Our Commander in Chief, Fidel Castro, will preside over a tactics meeting of the fifteen future liberators of the island of Cuba."

5

A camp and a sentry lookout were built in the mountains. The *rebeldes* tried to lie low while they organized themselves. Airplanes circled above the trees, searching futilely for ground prey like temporarily blinded hawks. Turret guns spattered ammunition, a bullet ripping Ché's shoulder. "Good practice," he told Fidel, "in cleaning a wound. Physician, heal thyself."

From mountainside huts five peasants provided food and were recruited as guerilla fighters. The peasants rode on horseback into nearby towns, bringing back guns, ammunition, and a shortwave radio. Ché and Fidel listened to radio reports from the mountain lookout. The student riot in Santiago de Cuba had been quashed by Batista. Students who had dynamited Havana's electric works

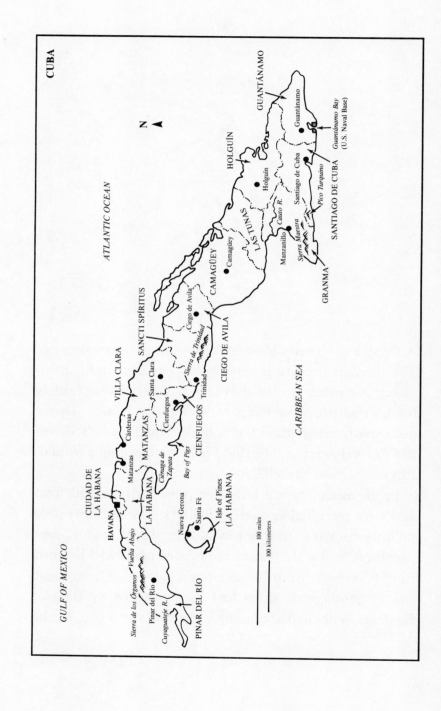

were dead, their bullet-ridden bodies tossed carelessly in a plaza.

The *rebeldes* reviewed what they had learned of Colonel Bayo's "minuet," a tactical dance to be used when battling a large army. In the minuet, guerillas would continually attack and withdraw, change position, attack and withdraw again. By moving from one base position to another, guerilla fighters could confuse and surprise the opposition. "Keep them guessing," Colonel Bayo had said. "Keep them shaking their heads."

On a Thursday the fifteen-plus guerillas weaved down a mountain route to attack a small garrison at the mouth of the La Plata River. Guns were confiscated while Ché and a Cuban, Luís Crespo, set the army post on fire. As the soldiers shot back, wounding three *rebeldes*, Ché immediately ripped shirts and socks into tourniquets and bandages.

Students, peasants, and political dissidents slowly appeared at the Sierra Maestra camp. They supplied more guns and were welcomed into the rebel army. On May 28, 1957, nine guerillas captured a garrison at El Uvero. For three hours the *rebeldes* shot streams of bullets from a hill overlooking the post. Ché toted a Magnum machine gun given to him by Fidel. At El Uvero, Fidel's promised mission impelling him, Ché was more fighter than doctor. "A new stage has begun for me," he wrote in a notebook from his knapsack.

The recovery of Fidel Castro's *rebeldes* did not go smoothly. For every ten recruits there were one or two desertions or deaths. Life in the mountains was harsh, and enemy aircraft and advancing soldiers made increasingly accurate hits. One Cuban guerilla lost an eye; another was disemboweled in an ambush. Colonel Bayo's minuet required setting up new positions, so constant ground clearing, trench digging, and camouflaging of equipment were necessary. Batista, furious that the guerillas hadn't collapsed, retaliated further. Frank Paíz, popular head of the student movement, was executed in Santiago de Cuba. Weeping crowds led by women and children jammed the streets to follow Paíz's casket, but Batista's police were ordered to shoot them down. For three days Santiago de Cuba was awash with spilled blood.

Again the guerillas rallied, and they opened a second base camp in the northern mountains. Their ranks swelled with Cubans dashing to take up arms against Batista's regime. In the name of the *rebeldes* the Cuban city of Cienfuegos was seized by a section of the navy that had defected from the government. Guerilla attacks against other garrisons and towns caused growing army casualties—and on November 9, 1957, one hundred bombs exploded in Havana's streets and plazas, set off by political dissidents.

The *rebeldes*, Batista was informed by his political advisors, had become a national movement. The Cuban people called the mountain camps "Free Territories." Major investors in Cuba and in the United States were questioning Batista's strength.

Enough! Fulgencio Batista raged. The rebel army must be thoroughly crushed. Its perpetrators and supporters

42

must be hung from gallows in Havana until their flesh rotted yellow in the blazing sun.

The full weight of Batista's military—fourteen army battalions flanked by the air force and the remaining navy—were hurled against the *rebeldes*. Within a month troops had retaken over ninety percent of guerilla-occupied territory. The men fighting for Fidel, now nearly three hundred in number, were once more a mere handful in comparison to the three thousand army soldiers. Ché hardly slept; he was endlessly prowling, plotting, checking casualties and supplies. Fidel appointed him comandante, the highest rank in the rebel army. His asthma was so fierce, he sometimes used his rifle butt as a crutch to keep upright. Urbano had helped lug him up a hill in the midst of mortar fire. Yet he was more resolute, dogged, and skillful than any of the other recruits. "Bayo was right," Fidel said. "You cough, Guevara, but you strike like a bandit."

By July 1958, despite the army's strength, the *rebeldes* had miraculously pulled themselves back from defeat. Speeding up the minuet, they came, as Ché had shouted aboard the *Granma*, like truth—unnerving and stark. By the twentieth of the month one guerilla column had converged on Santiago de Cuba, and two others on the cities of Mar Verde, Pino del Agua, and Minas del Frío. Hundreds of army soldiers surrendered. The radio in the first guerilla camp blared with the news that almost all opposition political parties in Cuba had signed a pact to support Fidel. Only the Communists abstained, wary of relinquishing any power.

In August Cuba's citizens were applauding the *rebeldes* and sabotaging government order. The guerillas, originally an unlikely thorn in Batista's side, were running riot over the island. On the slope of a mesa Ché helped Fidel use a stick to trace the final battle plan in the sandy dirt. Ché would be entrusted with bringing the revolution to absolute victory. He would lead one hundred fifty men over hundreds of miles to systematically sever communication between eastern and western coasts and to occupy the city of Santa Clara. The men under Ché's command would travel by truck, with maps. Springfield, Garand, and M-1 rifles, 30-caliber machine guns, and two bazookas were available.

The gasoline that was supposed to be delivered for the trucks was waylaid by Batista's soldiers. Undaunted, Ché told his men they would walk instead of ride. "Many of us," Ché said, "may not live to tell our story. But if just one of us does, he will help fulfill the purpose of our Commander in Chief, Fidel Castro."

The September and October march to Santa Clara—and the battle that followed—established Ché as a guerilla hero. Only four days in the woods he and his men were met by a tropical storm that flooded rivers and made roads impassable. Ché pushed the march through unyielding brush where mosquitoes descended in hordes. Distant but approaching gunfire warned him of enemy troops. For twelve days he restricted his men to night maneuvers. In daylight he ordered them to hide in caves or at the bottoms of ravines.

When days turned into rigorous weeks, the guerilla

casualties mounted from skirmishes with the army. The men began faltering. The drinking water was dirty; rocks tore boots into shreds and were ravaging feet. The guerillas, however, had an amazing example before them. Gasping for breath, wheezing as if his lungs were a broken machine, Ché was indomitable. He spared himself nothing. If rafts needed to be built to cross streams, he was first to take an axe to the trees. If rains pelted or suns scorched, it was he who resisted shelter or rest.

At last the guerillas had chopped, crawled, and hiked their way through the forests onto the famous Júcaro–Morón route defended by Cuban patriots in the War of Independence against Spain. Informed by two guerilla lookouts of an army ambush near the Júcaro River, Ché told his weary men to abandon the roads and to swim the river. They spent several weeks in the central Las Villas province, cutting railroad ties and wrecking bridges before tackling Santa Clara. In early December, inspired by Ché's endurance, the guerilla column bombed the bridge over the Falcón River at the Central Highway, halting land transport between Havana to the west and other Cuban cities to the east. What remained in the exhausting, four-month-old march was the taking of Santa Clara, the axis city of the central plain.

On December 29, 1958, unshaven and bearded like Fidel, Ché propelled his men onto Santa Clara's main streets. Many of the city's one hundred fifty thousand residents stayed indoors, peeking at the guerillas from behind shutters or waiting for gunfire. Ché set up a command post in the administration building of Santa Clara's university and dispatched squads of guerillas to occupy the factory district, business district, and residential area. Word was passed to him that Batista had sent an armored train of four hundred soldiers to defend the city. The prospect did not frighten him. "The train," he exulted, "can only travel on rails we haven't cut. It will have to stop in the station."

The train trap at Santa Clara was final proof of the revolution's victory and of the soon-to-be-legend of Ché Guevara. On December 30 the long, armored train halted in the rail yard as Ché led fifty guerillas with hastily made Molotov cocktails down to the tracks. *"Now!"* Ché shouted, swinging his arms in a wide arc. *"Throw now! Freedom soars in the name of the people!"*

The "cocktails," hurled at the train and detonating in burning masses of gasoline, forced most of Batista's soldiers out of the railroad cars and down the length of the platform. Gasping as Ché gasped, the soldiers were unable to run from the guerillas, who darted out, guns firing, from behind groups of tin sheds. Weaving back and forth in their dance, the guerillas followed Ché's signals and shouts. Soon all the soldiers, ashen faced, had bolted from the smoky train. "The armored cars," Ché would write, "became a veritable furnace for the soldiers. And in a few hours the whole complement surrendered with its twenty-seven cars, its antiaircraft guns, its machine guns of the same type, its fabulous quantities of ammunition."

The defeat was stunning. On New Year's Day, 1959, Santa Clara fell to Ché, the news thundering throughout the world. Batista was weary and depressed after twenty-

46

five months of failing to annihilate the guerillas or to smother a revolution that should have been doomed. Across the island thousands cheered the success of Fidel Castro and of his remarkable *rebeldes.* They excitedly hailed the Argentinian—wasn't his name *Ché?*—who had played the winning hand against Cuba's dictator. Batista fled to the Dominican Republic. Government officials and police officers without safe haven in Cuba scurried after him. *How did it happen?* they asked each other. *How could a band of upstarts, of discontents who'd come on an absurdly tiny boat, conquer a whole regime?*

On January 4, Ché was a dark flash among the pastel buildings of the city of Havana. He rode in an open car at the head of his victorious guerilla column. Spectators in smocks or wide-cuffed pants and shirts, a populace of supporters, called him hero. Fidel, the leader he'd followed, had asked him to remain in Cuba at his side. Standing up in the car, Ché silently honored the sixty-seven guerillas who had died among the sugarcane and the fifteen who regrouped to devour a dictatorship. He grinned at Urbano, who sat near the car door, and felt his chest ease long enough for one gloriously full, unshackled breath to give him air. At that moment in Havana, enemies within and without seemed to have ceased their assault. They would return, Ché knew—regrouped also, energized anew—but on that fourth day of the new year 1959 the daring revolution in Cuba and the unrest burning within him tasted sweet and benign in his mouth.

6

Alberto Granados was now a successful biochemist. Invited to Cuba by Ché, he flew in for the celebrations with Ché's mother. "My son," Celia boasted to personnel at Havana's Rancho Boyero Airport, "is a true liberator. He has made a stunning revolution!"

Ché noticed how thin his mother looked. Her cancer, however, had receded, and as usual she ignored the subject. Delivering news of her other children—their interests in politics or law—she spoke to her eldest son of opportunity. "You, Ernesto—'Ché'—will show the world how society can succeed without rulers and ruled. The working class is the great equalizer."

"Fidel and I," Ché said, "are reconstructing Cuban government. We make the United States nervous with our land reform. They say we are throttling free enterprise."

48

From Alberto Granados, Ché received greetings and congratulations sent from his father in Buenos Aires. "But where," Alberto asked as he and Ché stood on Havana's docks, "are your wife and daughter, Guevara, amid all this grand commotion?"

"They will be here soon," Ché answered slowly. "I will see my little girl. I've missed the hours of exchanging books and reciting poems with Hilda, but . . ."

"*But?*" Alberto asked.

"Is it only twenty-six months since I left Mexico?" Ché said. "Cuba consumes me."

Ché had been given a row of offices in the building that had housed the Ministry of War under Batista. He had hired a male secretary, Manresa, and a female assistant, Aleida March, but he refused most protocol. He wore creased khaki shirts with the collars turned inward and paratrooper boots over his pants. He worked and admitted visitors to his office from midnight to five or six A.M., sleeping through the mornings. A revolver hung from the holster on his belt.

Latin American countries were formally recognizing Cuba's new revolutionary government. By mid-January the United States and Great Britain joined the acceptance, and Fidel flew to the United States for meetings with Vice President Richard Nixon and Secretary of State Christian Herter. Fidel was warned about the "dangers of Cuban nationalism" and was refused his steep request for 30 billion dollars in Latin American aid, but he returned to Cuba in an exuberant mood. "We've made our mark," he said to Ché. "The U.S. is listening, even though they

Speaking to the Cuban people in Havana, Ché still wears his "uniform" from the legendary battles of the Cuban revolution. *AP/Wide World Photos.*

disagree with our tactics. I am taking the title of Prime Minister of Cuba. And you, my coughing guerilla-economist, will be Minister of Industries!"

Crowds of journalists followed Ché on the streets. Photographs of him appeared on the front pages of newspapers. The back-roads Argentine wanderer had become an instant celebrity. He had wanted a "voice," a way to argue the philosophies he believed to be true. On January 27, 1959, he offered a program to the Cuban people. Borrowing a phrase from Lenin, chairman and statesman of Russia's 1917 postrevolutionary government, he said that Cuba must be an "armed democracy." The revolutionary army, he explained, would serve as "vanguard of the people." Cuba's mines and telephone system would be nationalized; land reform would break up the estates of the rich. "Our brothers elsewhere in America," Ché said, "struggle as we did in the countryside, and from there carry the revolution to the cities. . . . The revolution is not limited to the Cuban nation. . . . Let this be the first step toward the victory of America."

Cuba's armed *rebeldes* were evident across Havana. They arrested army officers who'd carried out Batista's orders, imprisoning them in the underground cells of La Cabaña, a stone-and-wood fortress. Many officers were tried by Fidel's "revolutionary court" and shot at night in a plaza whose bloody walls showed craters of bullet scars. Ché took no pleasure in the deaths but called them revolutionary justice. In Guatemala he had witnessed the fall of a revolution when the army wouldn't support its new government against invading mercenaries. In Cuba officers who had been "too loyal" to Fulgencio Batista would not survive to sabotage Fidel Castro.

Learning to pilot a Cessna airplane, Ché flew over Cuba's sugarcane fields to study the island's dependence on agriculture. At the sight of the plane field-workers stopped swinging their machetes to wave in admiration. Yet Ché did not keep himself above the people. He led crews of three thousand, rich and poor, into the fields to chop cane. He drove himself past exhaustion with a machete as he'd done when heading his guerilla column, wheezing this time from the microscopic powder thrown off by the cane. "But look," he said proudly, "at the ability of different social classes to work together. The people can outpace any stiff-necked, bureaucratic dogma that separates the haves and have-nots."

The gun in Ché's holster was not used in the early months of 1959, although not every Cuban was a friend of the revolution. Rumbles sounded from stray anti-Castroites or from disgruntled old guard Communists. Fidel urged his comandante to keep a bodyguard, but Ché adamantly refused. "Safety lies in the mouth of *my* gun," he said, "not in the gun of a hired protector."

One gray predawn morning Ché left his office to walk toward the high stone walls of La Cabaña. He needed sleep, but his restlessness gnawed at him. At noon Hilda and Hildita would arrive at the airport. He'd said good-bye to his mother and to Alberto Granados on the same airport runway, Celia talking incessantly of progressive action and moral justice. Cuba could be free, he'd told her, of its groveling dependence on selling hundreds of thousands of tons of sugar to the United States. Cuba could be industrialized and self-supporting, dividing its wealth fairly among its citizens. He had risked his life for that vision—would risk it, if necessary, again.

He craned his neck to see La Cabaña's heavy rooftop, tensing over the remembered shrieks of those assassinated by order of Fidel's court. Imposed death, he reminded himself, was necessary . . . wasn't it? How could men have liberty except by destroying oppressors? How could passive resistance or peaceful negotiation—bloodless and merciful, to be sure—accomplish anything permanent? He and Fidel hadn't thrown mercy to the wolves, had they?

Ché used a key to let himself into La Cabaña, moving quietly toward the stairs that plummeted down to the cells. The corridors were musty; cracks marked the walls like dividing lines on a map. Unlocking another door, he shoved it open. But where, he wondered, were they—the nine or ten prisoners he'd expected to find sprawled across the floor? Emptiness greeted him—silence—until a throaty voice remarked, "*Dead*, Comandante Guevara. Everyone else is already dead."

Whirling toward his left, Ché glimpsed a shape propped limply against a pole. Dark, oval eyes assailed him. A thin arm lifted in salute. He didn't know the young man in open-necked black shirt and black pants, but some vague quality about him was familiar. "What is the reason for your arrest?" Ché asked.

"The usual," the prisoner said. "I was in President Batista's front guard. I'll be shot tomorrow. Spoils of war, no?"

53

Ché nodded. What was it, he kept puzzling, about this prisoner—the flat ridge of cheekbone, the probing stare? Then he knew. *Paolo!* Yes! The young man in black resembled Paolo, the boy he'd befriended in Peru's leper colony. The farewell in the prisoner's eyes—sadness overpowered by courage—matched Paolo's farewell as he had clung to the mast of the lepers' boat. "If you were free," Ché asked the prisoner, "what would you do?"

"Find another cause, Comandante," the young man said.

Ché could not squelch the impulse. *So,* he defended himself, *why not? Why not on this gray-tipped dawn? Save, release, create a different story. Make a convert for the revolution. Take a chance.* "Go!" Ché said, suddenly swinging the iron door backward until it squeaked on its hinges. "You! Prisoner! Get yourself *out* of here."

"You mean it?" the young man asked, his eyes alight, his shoulders jerking against his black shirt.

Ché stepped away from the door, unblocking the path of the Cuban dawn as it slipped through the well of an underground window. With a last glance at the chiseled face of prisoner-Paolo-himself, he said, "I always mean it."

What had changed in meaning for Ché was his marriage. Hilda was his friend and would remain so all her life, their bond being ideas more than romance. The "cause"—revolution—and the "foe"—imperialism—had been their guiding stars. Hildita, three years old and curious about her "Papá," made Ché smile with affection, but romance had unexpectedly bloomed for him after the Cuban revolution with a young and beautiful coworker who had served Fidel since the early attack on the Moncada Army Barracks.

Aleida March was Ché's twenty-two-year-old assistant, quiet but fiercely and surprisingly independent. She had smuggled clothes to the *rebeldes* in the Sierra Maestra camps, managing the steep climbs with ease, and had followed Ché and his column into Havana. "I want to marry her," Ché told Hilda in a Cuban café.

"It was clear from the start," Hilda said sadly, "that only the revolution must never really end."

"Can we remain friends?" Ché asked.

"Of course," Hilda said.

Divorced within a month, Ché married his young assistant on June 3, 1959, with Raúl Castro, Fidel's brother, as witness. Politics, and Ché's restlessness, were to cut short the honeymoon. He informed his wife, his ex-wife, and his daughter that he'd been given an assignment to travel as Cuba's spokesman. He left at once for Morocco, Japan, China, Indonesia, Ceylon, Pakistan, Yugoslavia, and the Sudan. Ceremoniously received by various heads of state, he carried his inhaler in his pocket. In China, suffering extreme asthma that almost halted the force of his words, he spent several hours with Mao Zedong, telling him that a revolutionary must combine an "impassioned spirit with coolness of mind."

"The most famous Argentine since Perón," Mao called him.

Ché brought picture postcards to little Hildita from his

As commander of La Cabaña fortress Ché helps determine which prisoners will go on trial. *AP/Wide World Photos.*

56

trip. Hilda, having decided to stay in Cuba, worked in the government's new land-reform agency. Aleida, three months pregnant, had set up housekeeping in a small cottage in Havana. Ché was glad to be home. He feasted with Aleida on her suppers of soups, meats, papayas, and gourds of mate. Even romance, however—even Aleida's heart-shaped face and soft curls of brown hair—did not stop him for long from stoking the revolution. In September, irritating the United States government, he arranged to sell three hundred thirty thousand tons of sugar to the Soviet Union. In November, though he was uncomfortable with money, he was appointed president of Cuba's National Bank to control finances with Fidel. On the first currency issued from his post, he signed his name "Ché," bypassing the formality of the "Guevara."

Over the next year Ché lived out a spectacular David-and-Goliath fantasy. From the bedridden days of his childhood, his wheezing an accompaniment or even a spur to his mother's political diatribes, to his talks with Hilda and Ricardo Rojo, *imperialismo yanqui* had been scorned. Any U.S. aid and benevolence toward Latin America— continuing funds and investments that helped reduce poverty by providing jobs, housing, and food—were summarily dismissed as worthless. U.S. factories, Ché believed, only ravaged local resources. U.S. support of dictators like Cuba's Batista or the Dominican Republic's Trujillo only caused pain. Using his position in Cuba, he began signing trade pacts with members of the Soviet bloc and with Communist China. He vented his anger at the United States by playing off the cold war between the U.S.

and the Soviet Union, between democracy and communism, impressing politicians everywhere by convincing Soviet Deputy Premier Anastas Mikoyan to confer with him in Havana and to grant Cuba a loan worth 1 million U.S. dollars.

The U.S. government denounced Fidel Castro's revolution as sabotaging the Cuban people. U.S. President Dwight D. Eisenhower called for economic sanctions against Cuba. Fearful of Soviet military aid to Castro, Eisenhower initiated surveillance flights over the island. Soon the situation was so grave that stories spread of a U.S. plan to invade Cuba. The United States, said its State Department, could not tolerate a possible Communist stronghold so close to its shores.

Replying by radio broadcast, Ché said that he had never been a member of the Communist Party, that he was an independent economist and thinker. "Free yourself from the imperialist's whip," he told Latin America's citizens by radio, "and the land you move across will be *your* land."

Ché was not only making speeches and trade pacts but writing as well. In May 1960 he published *Guerilla Warfare*, a book on revolutionary war that asked the "people's forces" to study his suggested program of military tactics. The book marked his broadening grasp of guerilla-army theory and strategy. Provoked by its theme, and by the arrival in Cuba of twenty-eight thousand tons of Soviet weapons, the U.S. severed diplomatic relations with Cuba on January 3, 1961. "Keep a hand on that gun of yours,"

Fidel told Ché. "Plots thicken against guerilla heroes who speak and write their minds."

In February Ché was to be officially sworn in as Cuban Minister of Industries. Aleida had given birth to a daughter, naming her Aleidita, and was expecting a second child. She invited Hilda and Hildita to join her on the huge platform in the plaza where Ché would be honored. Meeting before the ceremony, the two families gathered in the front yard of the cottage where Ché and Aleida lived. Five-year-old Hildita, wearing her "party dress," clung to her father's arm. Both mothers chatted amiably with each other while Aleidita gurgled from her stroller.

Ché and his secretary, Manresa, walked into the sunlit street. Their shadows stretched sideways toward the intersection of Séptima Avenida and Décimoctava Calle. "This is a fine day for you, Comandante," Manresa said. "President of the National Bank and now Minister of Industries. You and Premier Castro are Cuba's benefactors. Even the United States doesn't frighten you."

"It is best, Manresa," Ché answered, inhaling against a spasm in his chest, "not to let anything or anyone make you afraid."

Turning toward the cottage, Ché gestured for Aleida and Hilda to bring the children to him. But as his fingers arched forward, a burst of gunfire marked his movements. Gunshots crackled past him, sending a nearby bird into a frenzied curve. Hurtling downward to the ground, he felt Manresa fling himself over him like a shield. "Bullets!" Manresa screeched. "An assassination attempt!"

59

Ché's elbows and left cheek stung from the impact of flesh on pavement. He was not surprised by the bullets; Fidel had warned him. He waited until the gunfire stopped, until the only sounds were of Hilda's weeping. Then, sliding out from under a trembling Manresa, he jumped up and brushed off clumps of mud on his hands. No one was hurt. Behind him, Aleida and Hilda were rushing at him with the children. The street showed no signs of the assassin. "Everything is all right," he said, drawing his gun from his holster. "It's time for us to appear at the plaza."

Aleida's face was pale above the firm set of her jaw. Winking at her, Ché joked about the failed assassin. Wasn't Ché Guevara, he said, still alive and kicking—still to be sworn in as Minister of Industries? Hadn't his book on guerilla warfare talked of being a "crusader for the people's freedom," a fighter who was "part of the very soil on which he fights"? Well, then, so be it—mud and all. Death had been sent reeling down Séptima Avenida like a drunken and shabby bum.

Taking Aleida's arm as Manresa pushed the baby's stroller, Hilda and Hildita walking beside him, Ché stepped resolutely toward the corner. His gun was poised in his hand, but he knew he would be dealing more directly with death another day—when death was far more serious and sober.

7

Did Ché go looking for trouble? Facing enemies had always let him thumb his nose at weakness, had vaulted him out of childhood vulnerability, had promised him strength. Rebellion had come with each defiant breath, beckoning him in a school inkwell or on a cart with a man with no legs, marching on the streets of Buenos Aires and Guatemala, speeding him across the seas to Cuba. As Minister of Industries Ché might have played it safe, but he kept goading the United States. In time he would clash with the Soviet Union and even with his friend and leader, Fidel.

Reports on Ché's desk in Havana had disclosed that several 1961 bombings across Santiago de Cuba were traced to saboteurs hired in the United States. Other reports detailed U.S. oil refineries in Cuba—Shell, Esso, and

Texaco—refusing to refine Cuban oil. Journalists continued pursuing Ché. Did he think, they asked, that Cuba would really be invaded by the United States? Did he believe that the new U.S. president, John F. Kennedy, would authorize an attack or try, instead, to improve U.S.–Cuban relations?

The journalists were answered on April 17, 1961, when fourteen hundred U.S.-armed-and-financed exiles landed by boat in Cuba's Bay of Pigs. Ché immediately flew from Havana to the nearby Zapata Peninsula, ordering mobilization there of air-transported *rebeldes*. In a matter of hours he was plotting ambush and counterattack. With his old guerilla cohort Urbano at his heels he found himself back in marshland, covered with mosquitoes. The invasion—the trouble—energized him. In forty-eight hours the disorganized exiles were overcome, and Ché was almost disappointed. The marshland under his boots had felt more pleasing to him than the marble of government halls.

In Havana Ché drove a giggling Hildita into the ticker-tape parade celebrating the Bay of Pigs victory. Hildita was jumping up and down in the car, but suddenly she crumpled forward into a fit of coughing. "Hildita!" Ché said in alarm. "Are you ill?"

"I cough like you, Papá," the child answered.

"I will drive you home," Ché said, stroking her shoulder. "We will call your mother."

Hildita lay in bed with a critically high fever. Ché bought a small bottle of camphor rub, heating spoonfuls of the brown jelly in the same sort of saucepan Celia had used. "Let her breathe the fumes," he advised a worried Hilda. "And tell my daughter that if she wishes to mimic her father, she should study revolution—not asthma."

Hildita recovered and was visited by Ché's second family: Aleida, Aleidita, and two more babies, Camilo and Celia. Since the crisis had passed, Ché would leave on a new assignment. He was to attend an international conference, the Alliance for Progress, planned by President Kennedy at the beach resort of Punta del Este, Uruguay. U.S. prestige had dropped after the Bay of Pigs fiasco, and to save face, Kennedy wanted to raise funds for poverty-stricken areas of Latin America. Ché reserved the entire second floor of Punta del Este's Plaza Hotel for himself, his guards, and his typists. He invited Celia, his mother, to fly in from Buenos Aires. "Other delegations are clamoring to see us," he'd told her by Havana telephone.

The Alliance for Progress conference was a huge intermingling of presidents, prime ministers, cabinet heads, support staffs; political intrigue filled the halls. On the highway between Montevideo and Punta del Este, Ché was welcomed by thousands of factory workers saluting him. On his first day at the hotel he met secretly with Arturo Frondizi and Janio Quadros, presidents of Argentina and Brazil, to discuss Soviet interest in Cuba and in various Latin American countries. Frondizi and Quadros admired Ché but were wary of hurting their U.S. ties. The U.S.–Cuban conflict had grown so large that, several weeks after the Alliance for Progress conference, Ché's continued visits to the two leaders caused political crises in Argentina and Brazil, soon forcing Frondizi and Quadros to resign.

Ché's most unlikely meeting in Punta del Este was with President Kennedy's assistant Richard N. Goodwin at a hotel cocktail party. Goodwin had helped mastermind the Bay of Pigs invasion. "Thank you for the attack," Ché said to him over a plate of oysters. "It consolidated the major elements in Cuba behind Fidel Castro."

Ché told Richard Goodwin that Cuba might consider limiting trade pacts with "the East" if the United States would lift its trade embargo and recognize Cuba's Marxist-Socialist leanings. Curtly, Goodwin agreed to carry Ché's offer to the White House but later issued a memo stating that the U.S. government "did not pursue the Guevara initiative."

Ché talked glowingly of Cuba at Punta del Este. Only Celia, seated by him in the conference hall, knew that crippling asthma had struck him once more. For a day he wheezed in heaving spasms in his hotel room, shutting the windows against the humid Uruguayan air. But waving off Celia's concern, he returned to the meeting tables. Nothing could stop him from criticizing President Kennedy's ten-year, $20-billion aid plan for Latin America. "Not enough!" he rasped. "Latin America's poor need thirty billion simply to stay alive."

Ché did not deal with the inconsistency of his criticism. Hadn't he been the one to prod Cuba toward economic freedom from the United States? The chance, however, to tackle his Goliath was just too tempting to him; besides,

64

his views on international responsibility had solidified. Superpowers such as the United States, he told the Alliance for Progress delegates, must totally commit themselves, regardless of cost, to less privileged countries. Men everywhere must offer a selfless sacrifice for the common welfare.

When the Alliance for Progress conference ended, Ché traveled through Europe and Africa with his "people's battle cry." If he wasn't crawling through mountain brush or jungle, he could stalk enemies elsewhere. Bewildering the ever-present journalists, he began lambasting the Soviet Union as well as the United States. The U.S.S.R., he said, was soft on capitalism. It hypocritically involved itself in peaceful coexistence with the United States. Moral and physical revolution had no room for such a "tacit accomplice" of "greedy imperialism."

Ché was photographed in one country after another— Yugoslavia, Algeria, Guinea, Ghana, Tanzania, Egypt. His wrinkled uniform, scuffed boots, and gun-filled holster were easily recognizable on newspaper pages; he had created an indelible image for himself. Quoted in articles and editorials, he expressed his political opinions as vehemently as he had his strategies on guerilla warfare. One Monday, at a news conference, he gave damning criticism of the United States; the next day he called the Soviets moral cowards. "You've gone too far," Fidel told him angrily when he returned to Cuba. "Lay off the Soviets, Guevara. We need our friends."

Why sell out? Ché had asked Fidel. To appease the powerful and to betray the victimized? The next October he again denounced the Soviets without consulting Fidel. Soviet Premier Nikita Khrushchev had supplied forty-two missiles to Cuba, receiving written warning from the United States. The missiles, said the U.S., were unacceptable. They must be removed. Within hours Khrushchev had ordered a crew to transport the missiles back onto Soviet ships. Outraged, Ché called the act "sabotage" against Cuba. Even the press, Ché said, was reporting that, confronted by Kennedy, Khrushchev had "blinked first."

By late 1964 Ché was traveling to Geneva, Switzerland, to speak at the World Conference on Trade and Development. From Geneva he went to Algiers to confer with President Ahmed Ben Bella on third world, or underdeveloped, nations; then to the United States to speak for Cuba at the United Nations and on the TV program *Face the Nation.* His relationship with Fidel—the man whom he'd respected above all others—was in serious jeopardy. Fidel, Ché felt, was losing the love of revolution in favor of rigid stability and structure. In turn, Fidel and his economic staff blamed Ché for shortages in consumer goods caused by the revolutionary government's too-rapid nationalization of existing industries. Ché was given little credit for the schools, hospitals, and factories that, planned and supervised by him, were being constructed all over the island.

In January 1965 Fidel handed Ché a mailed invitation from Algeria's Ben Bella that asked the Cuban Minister of Industries to appear at the Organization of Afro-Asian Solidarity in Algiers. "Go," Fidel said, "as long as you don't use the conference for your ill-advised grievances against the Soviets. Keep your mouth shut, Guevara, when it counts."

Ché's stomach knotted over the words he wasn't supposed to say. Flying to Algiers, he stood on a podium and stared down at a group of African and Mideastern leaders. He'd realized that he could remind the men of the link between all human beings who were hungry and poor. He could urge them to set explicit goals for the development of their countries. But how could he swallow not showing his audience its enemies? Shouldn't the world's devils be named? Shouldn't even the Cuba he'd helped build be damned for its growing bureaucratic stance? If he was afraid of anything, it was of turning the other cheek.

Nodding at President Ben Bella, Ché made a swift decision. Maybe he would dig his own political grave with Fidel, and with Soviet Premier Khrushchev, over what he would say, but . . . *tough.* Nothing had ever stopped him from vaulting into whatever chaos he chose.

He coughed and cleared his throat. Stronger nations, he told his audience in a loud voice—in *his* voice—must lift the weaker onto their backs. He had traveled to Algiers to publicly repeat that, first, the United States did not meet its obligations to less fortunate countries and that, second, neither did the Soviet Union. Soviet help, he explained brusquely, was stingily meted out and sometimes ripped away. An extreme shake-up must occur in world economics. Everyone should use whatever means possible—even force, if necessary—to pressure richer nations into dividing and sharing their goods and services among the disadvantaged. He was drawing upon socialist Karl Marx's maxim "From each according to his abilities, to each according to his needs." New revolutions must come. Former methods had not succeeded.

Ché paused to assess the murmurs and objections from the men in the room. He seemed to be irritating his audience. Well, he thought, he had never taken the popular path, had he? The world's sicknesses would not be cured by half-baked or moderate measures. He was compelled to overthrow, overturn—to rail against what *was* for what *could be*.

He finished speaking to polite applause only from President Ben Bella. Carefully the several dozen diplomats and leaders in their business suits and frowns left the assembly hall and filed into the lobby. Ché wanted to run after them, to shout, "Listen! The future of your own countries is at stake. Listen before it's too late!" But *would* they listen? He had won recognition throughout the world as the daring revolutionary who had helped free 8 million Cuban people from their shackles. His attention had been sought by presidents and kings. Yet he was also a foreigner in foreign lands, the unruly, reckless Cuban radical who was not even Cuban.

He stood alone on the podium in Algiers, a lock of his hair falling darkly across his forehead. His presence itself was a demand for action. For many who knew Ché or had read of him, he reached too far and dreamed too rashly, pursuing discord at any cost. For Ché Guevara himself, however, his reach and his dreams were always a constant and sustaining imperative. They would remain so, even if they might ultimately exceed his grasp.

68

8

On April 12, 1965, at one of Ché's scheduled outings, Cuban officials gathered in Camagüey, west of Havana, to cut sugarcane with the field-workers. Ché was not present. On April 18, at the funeral of César Escalante, an old guard Cuban Communist who'd supported the *rebeldes*, Ché was not seen. And on May 18, when Celia de la Serna de Guevara unexpectedly died of her cancer, her eldest son did not attend her burial.

The journalists flew in curiosity to Cuba, then to Algeria, Russia, mainland China. Ché was nowhere in sight. Even Aleida and Hilda, both mourning Celia, could offer no explanation. Aleida, mother now of four Guevara children—Aleidita, Camilo, Celia, and baby Ernesto—sat surrounded by newspapers, the daily repositories of news

69

about Ché. Headlines read: IS CHÉ ILL?; IS CHÉ GUEVARA DEAD?; IS CHÉ ON A NEW MISSION?

Questions descended on Fidel from telephones and telegraph machines across Latin America, Europe, and the United States. Manresa, Ché's secretary, was assigned to issue the vague responses. But as spring became summer, Ché's whereabouts remained unknown. The newspapers began publishing excerpts from his guerilla warfare book. His old test scores from medical school were printed and analyzed; his personal library of poets, historians, and philosophers was reviewed. One editorial said that Ché Guevara was an avenger for social justice who had liked to pull the rug out from under the established "big boys." Ché, said the editorial, was the Argentine who hadn't "gone home," the comandante who wouldn't hang up his uniform. He stood politically at odds with twentieth-century luminaries such as Martin Luther King, civil rights advocate, and Mahatma Gandhi, resistor against British imperialism, who had preached nonviolent social change. Ché was heir to Simón Bolívar's adage: "To hesitate is to perish."

Through the summer and winter of 1965 Fidel did not officially comment on Ché's absence. He dismissed the local headlines that demanded, ¿DONDE? ¿DONDE ESTÁ?—"Where? Where is he?" He sidestepped the rumors that Ché had been discovered practicing medicine in Brazil, was piloting a helicopter in Vietnam, had been murdered in an uprising in the Dominican Republic. Only when the public uproar escalated into bedlam did Fidel release a statement. Comandante Guevara, said Fidel, was

70

"always where he will be most useful to the revolution."

In truth, Ché had voluntarily washed himself from Fidel's hair by dropping out of view. He hadn't wanted to keep embarrassing his friend, but neither was he willing to stifle himself. He would move on, he'd decided—leave Cuba permanently, establish a base and a new revolution elsewhere. His family, promised education and employment by Fidel, would stay in Havana. He would have liked to be near Aleida and the children, but Cuba was a burned bridge behind him, and he needed the fires of change rather than established routine. He had given Fidel a written outline of his plans. First he would vanish from sight, flying temporarily into the leftist Afro-Cuban camp that operated in Africa's Congo. Then, with Fidel's agreement and backing, he would select a site somewhere in Latin America, a location ripe for guerilla maneuvers. He would organize all warfare operations in the chosen *foco*, using Cuban guns, ammunition, and money. He would be lent two dozen of the best *rebeldes*, some from Africa, some from Cuba. *Would Fidel agree? Yes*, Fidel had said.

In March 1965, a month after his impassioned speech in Algeria, Ché left Cuba. He told no one but Fidel of his scheduled airplane flight to Brazzaville in the Congo. He had simply disappeared, disguised by fake eyeglasses, dyed hair, and a pillow stuffed under his shirt to make him look fatter. He was deep in the Congo when his mother died; the news had not penetrated the jungle. By then, two of his Cuban *rebeldes*, Pombo Tamayo and Tuma Cuello, were scouting locations for him in Peru, Bolivia, and Argentina, sending long reports that eventually reached the

71

African camp. The men had found a site in the remote Ñancahuazú River valley of southeast Bolivia, the country where, twelve years before, Ché had witnessed the political victory of the MNR. Now the movement had lost power to a repressive military regime. Poverty and disease were rampant, with miners in the mining centers rebelling against the government and against U.S. involvement in Bolivian politics. Sales of tin, the country's only major export, were dangerously low.

Ché wired Pombo and Tuma that the Ñancahuazú Valley could be an ideal *foco* and that he would fly at once into La Paz, Bolivia, by a circuitous route through Czechoslovakia and East Germany. It was November 1966 when he waited to be picked up by jeep in a clearing in Brazzaville, disguised again by eyeglasses, dyed hair, and pillow. In his knapsack were two letters that he'd written and had planned to mail from Prague, Czechoslovakia. In the clearing, dry reeds crackling under his boots, he felt suddenly and comfortingly ready for his next trouble, for whatever might lie ahead in Bolivia's tropical valley. If he sensed, on some deeper level, a tightening clutch on his breath and his life, he revealed it only through several lines in the letters he would mail. To his children, he had said, "Dear Hildita, Aleidita, Camilo, Celia, and Ernesto: Grow up like good revolutionaries. . . . Remember that the revolution is the important thing and that each of us, alone, is worth nothing. . . ."

And to the traveling companion of his more footloose days, Alberto Granados, Ché had written, "My rolling

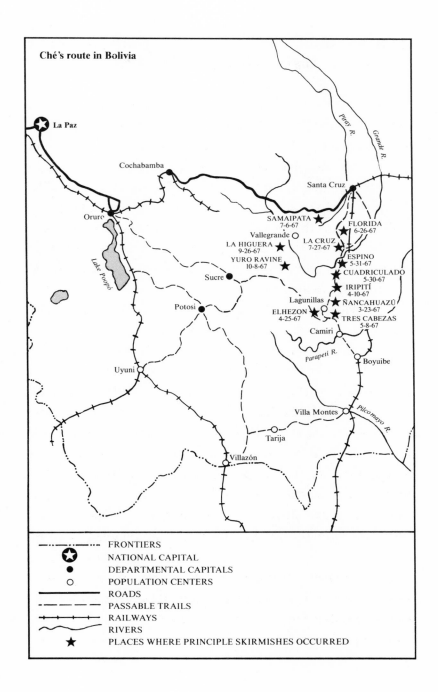

Ché's route in Bolivia

La Paz

Cochabamba

Piray R.

Grande R.

Santa Cruz

Orure

SAMAIPATA ★
7-6-67

FLORIDA ★
6-26-67

Vallegrande ○

LA CRUZ ★
7-27-67

LA HIGUERA ★
9-26-67

ESPINO ★
5-31-67

YURO RAVINE ★
10-8-67

CUADRICULADO ★
5-30-67

Lake Poopó

Sucre ●

IRIPITÍ ★
4-10-67

Lagunillas ○

ÑANCAHUAZÚ ★
3-23-67

Potosi ●

ELHEZON ★
4-25-67

TRES CABEZAS ★
5-8-67

Camiri ○

Parapeti R.

Boyuibe ○

Uyuni ○

Villa Montes ○

Pilcomayo R.

Tarija ○

Villazón ○

— · · — · · — FRONTIERS

✪ NATIONAL CAPITAL

● DEPARTMENTAL CAPITALS

○ POPULATION CENTERS

——— ROADS

— — — — PASSABLE TRAILS

+‑+‑+‑+‑+ RAILWAYS

‿‿‿‿ RIVERS

★ PLACES WHERE PRINCIPLE SKIRMISHES OCCURRED

house has two legs once again and my dreams have no frontier—at least until the bullets speak."

Twenty-one guerillas had come to Bolivia, split by Ché into two platoons. Leading eleven of the men along a twist of the Rio Grande, he listened for the other ten. He had put the second platoon under the command of Joaquín, a Cuban who had fought for nine months in Vietnam. The Ñancahuazú terrain was so impassable, however, that visibility was less than six feet. Joaquín and his guerillas were somewhere in the thorny liana, vine, and smothering bushes. Any sounds they might have made were drowned out by the crash of rapids in the river.

Ché had organized a twenty-eight-day march for the platoons, a scouting expedition across the valley to learn its mountains, forests, and canyons. Heavy rainfall had dogged the men from the first day. Rocks had ripped shoes and razor-sharp cacti had punctured skin. With a machete and axe, Ché had assumed front position, hacking paths through the vegetation. He was keeping a new notebook to summarize daily maneuvers. On December 12 he wrote of teaching his men " 'the facts of life' on the realities of war." Their mission, he'd said, might take seven to ten years to grow strong enough to bring power to the Bolivian people—and to overthrow the existing government.

Ché's march through the Ñancahuazú Valley had slowly bogged down to nearly twice its scheduled length. Rain-soaked maps from La Paz had proved unreliable, and the platoons continually lost their way. On the morn-

74

ing of March 19 Ché counted only two remaining cans of food. His men—Pombo, Tuma, Urbano, Rolando, Ricardo, Pacho, Luís, Benigno, Marcos, Miguel, and Aniceto—sat stiff legged on a machete-cleared circle of ground. Faces were tense, eyes heavy lidded. Shirts and jackets were stained with mildew, hanging in tatters. Ché's own shirt was blotched with the phlegm that he coughed up day and night. Never had his chest burned so badly or his lungs strained so for air. But asthma and his new revolution had merged for him into a dual battle to breathe free. His platoon might not be showing the best vigor of the guerilla fighter, but the men had withstood a long, arduous march. "In the beginning," he'd read to them from his warfare book, "the essential thing for the guerilla is to not let himself be destroyed."

Since arriving in Bolivia, Ché and his men had not been discovered by the regular army. They had built a base camp on a remote farm purchased with Fidel's money. Neighboring peasants were scarce; reports indicated that there were on the average only three residents per square mile of land. The guerillas had hidden a radio transmitter in a cave on the farm, covering it with branches. Digging a series of tunnels in a ravine, they buried tools, guns, rifles, ammunition, food, and medicine. Seven of the recruits followed directions in Ché's book to construct log tables, benches, a latrine, and a mud oven for baking bread.

Now, searching for the second platoon at the Rio Grande, Ché called out for his weary men to move faster. He knew that he had to keep the guerillas on their feet in order to locate Joaquín's platoon. Too many days had passed away from the base camp. Tempers were short, and a bout of diarrhea had done damage. Some nights, in frustration, the men had become aware that they'd crawled, hacked, and sweated all day long only to make a path that circled back to their morning campsite.

"We're trying to maintain your pace, Comandante," Urbano grumbled at Ché, buttoning his frayed jacket. "But the men are hungry."

Ché meted out the few remaining crusts of stale bread. He scanned the trees for a blackbird or two that might provide a real breakfast, but no satiny wings flashed from the green leaves. He had talked to the men about hunger, about that churning in the stomach that had led Bolivia's Indians to chew the numbing coca leaves that grew across much of the country's almost half million square miles. In La Paz he had observed the same hollow-eyed, hungry stare that he'd seen elsewhere in Latin America—the walking death of a people smothered by their leaders. Swinging his machete in a shoulder-throbbing arc, he chopped at a web of vines, liquid slapping into his face. Latin America, he thought, *must* undergo change—bit by bit, chop by chop, spurred by the revolution.

In an hour Ché and his platoon finally stumbled onto enough familiar landmarks to determine that their winding, forty-eight-day march was actually at end. The canyon walls at the river were sticky with heat. Rummaging through his knapsack for his empty inhaler, Ché held the useless glass bulb upside down, spraying only a puff of stale air into his mouth, a gesture that had become automatic to him in the scorching valley. Couldn't one drop of adrenaline have lingered in the inhaler and rolled toward the nozzle, allowing itself to be squeezed outward? "Rest, why don't you," Tuma had told him above his wheezing of the last day as the platoon was about to cross the Rio Grande on a makeshift raft.

"I'll have plenty of time to rest," Ché had answered, his chest heaving, "when I'm no longer around."

An air-hungry dizziness lodged behind his eyes. He dropped the inhaler into his shirt and swung his machete even harder. The asthma, he thought, could go to hell. He was not going to rest. A dozen more guerillas, recruited by a tin miner from the town of Oruro, should be waiting at the camp. Joaquín and the other platoon might have returned. The revolution would swell its ranks with peasants and miners. Daily maneuvers, even more marches, could secretly train and harden the men in preparation for a first attack on the unsuspecting army.

Chopping at clumps of bushes, Ché suddenly signaled to Ricardo and Urbano, who followed at his heels. Ahead, like a welcoming palm, was the edge of the ravine that abutted the Ñancahuazú farm. The camp was only yards away; food and medicine were in the caves. "Target!" Ché yelled, his voice hoarse, his throat aching.

Yet as he quickened his pace, Ché heard—and then saw—an airplane dipping and hovering overhead. Military markings covered the silver tail, the significance undeniable. Bolivia's army had discovered the isolated guerilla camp; the cat was out of the bag. Instantly, Ché realized that sufficient training of his men was no longer

77

possible. The initial contact between his guerilla platoons and the regular army would occur much sooner than he'd hoped. "Not at all a good omen," he would write tersely on that March 19, 1967, in his Bolivian notebook.

9

The first combat—death's military dance—happened in the early hours of March 23. Having moved to a hastily readied second base camp, Ché's platoon ambushed a thirty-two man army patrol near the Ñancahuazú River. Ché was keenly aware not only that some of his men were undertrained, and that he hadn't located the second platoon, but also that he had no support yet among the peasants of the region. He could have retreated to the forests, playing for time, keeping his identity secret, but retreat didn't tempt him. Kneeling beside a tree on March 23, he fired his gun seconds ahead of the other guns, as if a baton in his hand were ushering in the next cascade of ricocheting sound.

The combat ended quickly, part of the patrol fleeing over a ridge. Seven army soldiers were killed, four wounded, nine taken prisoner. The guerillas obtained sixteen army rifles, three machine guns, and two bazookas. "A precise and spectacular attack," Ché would write, calling the Bolivian patrol "totally ineffective."

The next day Ché released the prisoners, stripping them of their uniforms and letting them scramble off in undershorts. Weeks would pass before he would hear that, to avoid ridicule from their superiors, the prisoners had exaggerated the size of the guerilla band. "We were completely overtaken by an infiltrating force," they'd raved, their story grabbed up and printed by the news services. "Guerillas everywhere! In the ravines, on the canyon tops. At least five hundred men!"

To retaliate, Bolivia's president, General Barrientos, ordered the Commander in Chief of the Air Force, Colonel Kolle, to send two thousand soldiers into the Ñancahuazú Valley. Helicopter guns strafed the area; CIA agents converged on La Paz; American Green Berets, a highly trained outfit of the U.S. military, flew in to help toughen Bolivian troops. Ché and his men were grateful now for the thick leaves and vines in the ravines and arroyos. Days passed, with the guerillas carefully breaking trails and hunting for food. Evenings involved Ché's teaching military tactics and organizing "win over the peasants" lessons in the Quechua language.

The plan, Ché said, was for the guerillas to grow in number and to hit at far points across the valley, forcing the Bolivian Army to disperse and weaken itself. When needed, the guerillas could withdraw to the second base camp for supplies. Then the movement would go north, over the mountains from La Paz to strike at the agricultural center, Cochabamba, then to the cities of Santa Cruz and Camiri to sever railroad lines and to cut the pipeline owned by the U.S.'s Gulf Oil. Finally the Bolivian revolution would spread to bordering countries—Argentina, Brazil, Chile, Peru—forcing the United States to honor its treaties to defend the Western Hemisphere. U.S. troops would be committed to Latin America, creating a "new Vietnam," a new and violent upheaval.

In early April, just north of the March 23 ambush site, the guerillas attacked a patrol in the region of Iripití. Rubio, a former captain of the *rebeldes*, was walking beside the Ñancahuazú River when he was shot. Angrily the guerillas discovered and set upon a fifteen-man patrol. Eleven casualties were inflicted on the army: one dead, three wounded, two of them dying afterward, and seven taken prisoner. Weapons and ammunition were seized. Ché would write that Rubio, legs twitching, lay "next to a wounded man; he was already in his death throes; his Garand was jammed, and a grenade was beside him, its pin pulled but unexploded."

Ché buried Rubio in a shallow grave, remarking somberly that the first guerilla blood spilled in the Bolivian revolution was Cuban. Not answering, Marcos and Pacho were arguing over a can of condensed milk as Benigno, his eyes badly infected, wiped his face with leaves. Ché tossed piles of dirt onto Rubio's grave. Beyond the mud-streaked circle of guerillas was the starkness of canyons and mountains. To Ché the civilized world seemed too distant to occupy the same planet as the Ñancahuazú Valley. He had

81

heard from army prisoners that newspaper reporters had followed troops into the guerillas' first base camp, but he hadn't seen a newspaper in months. The radio transmitter that had been the main contact with Fidel in Havana was ruined beyond repair by water seepage, and any peasants encountered on mountain paths were polite but obviously wary. The isolation of the river valley was becoming the isolation of the guerillas, a second ominous note in Ché's Bolivian mission.

In April he sent a message to Fidel through a contact from La Paz who had made his way into the second base camp. The message described both successful attacks on the army and a happy reunion in the camp with Joaquín and the second platoon. Using a code and invisible ink, Ché said that the revolution was in its "consolidation and purification" stage. Some desertions had occurred, and the MNR had not offered the guerillas any help because of its fears of General Barrientos and because of ties to the United States. The Bolivian Communist Party had notified the La Paz contact of wanting leadership of Ché's revolution, but Ché had refused their demands. However, he'd told Fidel in seeming nonconcern, there would be other support. "The finest and most combative people," he said, "will be on our side."

On April 18 the guerillas—now forty-two in number after the arrival of new volunteers—marched southward to the town of Matajal. Two men lagged behind: Alejandro, a Cuban, gripped by spasms of diarrhea that stained his pants, and Moisés, a Bolivian miner, who was retching. A hard rain fell, soaking jackets until they lay like weights

82

across shoulders. By a thatched *bohío*, or hut, Ché motioned to his men. He presented himself to the hut's owner, a Señor Padilla. No need to fear, he reassured the uneasy peasant. The guerillas meant to aid Bolivia's Indians and to persuade General Barrientos to befriend them also.

Señor Padilla, speaking in Spanish, not Quechua, gave the guerillas corn and potatoes inside the hut—for which Ché insisted on paying—but he was still not friendly. "Wouldn't you like to live a better life?" Ché asked, seeing the broken chairs tilting on the dirt floor and the baby, half naked, nose dripping, who chewed on a red worm.

"General Barrientos will not forget the peasants," Señor Padilla answered.

"But you have hardships," Ché said. "Rich and greedy leaders plunder your country and steal what is yours. If you and your friends join us, we will act together to claim shoes, clothes, medicines, and land. We will create a government to protect you, not smother you. We must fight for liberty. It will not fall into our laps. The whole world soon will be watching what happens in Bolivia."

Señor Padilla nudged his straw hat over his forehead, digging into a pocket of his trousers for a coca leaf. A guinea pig scuttled across the floor. Chewing on the leaf, its juice a narcotic, the peasant muttered, "You're the ones hunted by the army. You want me to fight with you. There are enough dead in Bolivia."

Hearing a cough—*was it his own?*—Ché turned toward an older child stretched out behind a fire pit. The child, a boy, was flushed crimson with fever. Ché ducked be-

83

neath two rusted kettles suspended above the pit and knelt down. He stroked the boy's forehead while he uttered a few reassuring words in Spanish and in Quechua. Considering the possibility of the child's having appendicitis, he pressed on the distended stomach. Then he put an ear to the sunken chest, listening for the heavy congestion of pneumonia. When he peered into the boy's crusted mouth, he found his answer—a rough, gray-colored membrane covering tonsils and uvula. "Diphtheria," Ché said aloud. "This could have been prevented by vaccine."

The boy, staring at Ché's wrinkled uniform and dusty gun, began crying. His cough worsened and his eyes bulged with fright. "My son nearly died last night," Señor Padilla said woodenly. "Choked until he was blue."

The boy was choking now, chest wracked by spasms. Staring down, Ché was suddenly seeing old faces again— Paolo, ill with leprosy in Peru, and the black-shirted young man he'd set free from the cell in La Cabaña. He lunged forward, grabbing the choking boy and prying open his mouth, shoving a hand toward the throat. As his fingers touched rough, scaly membrane, he yanked, tearing the film away. The boy screamed, blood spurting onto his tongue, but his choking had stopped.

"I'm a doctor," Ché rasped at Señor Padilla. "Your son will probably live. I have pills in my knapsack for him, but he needs stronger medicine. You must take him to a hospital."

"Hospitals turn peasants away," Señor Padilla answered. "Beds go to military, government, and industry."

"Then you *understand*!" Ché said at once, gripping the

man's shoulder. "General Barrientos does, indeed, forget the peasants! Lend the guerillas your support! Let us help you and your country."

Señor Padilla stepped backward. "No," he said sourly. "You have helped my son. I thank you. But I want you to go. I don't want you here."

Frowning, Ché opened his knapsack and plucked out a smeared bottle of pills. He had not expected such suspicion from Bolivia's peasants. He had thought they would be eager for a spokesman. Change, however, seemed to terrify them. Had they all become zombies? Were they so numbed to pain and to a walking death-sleep that even a sick child, relieved of diphtheria's suffocating membrane, could not startle any of them awake?

Disheveled towns and hamlets, peopled sparsely by peasants, dotted the guerillas' "minuet" through southeastern Bolivia. Matajal became Muyupampa, Taperillas, Ticucha, Mesón. At Yacuiba, near Santa Cruz, Ché's platoon set up an ambush. Three soldiers were killed, one wounded.

Publicity, supplied partly by Radio Havana, continually exaggerated the number of guerillas but not their successes against Bolivian troops. Journalists who had searched for Ché since his mysterious disappearance, and heads of state who had watched his outlaw politics, were considering that Ché Guevara might be the leader of Bolivia's guerilla war. Fidel finally released an article entitled "To Create Two, Three . . . Many Vietnams, That Is the Slogan," datelined "From Somewhere in Latin America" by Ché. The piece prompted widespread agreement that Ché was alive. Soon Havana distributed a Ché Guevara "Manifesto" and four photographs showing him, uniformed, in the jungle. Ché watchers, said the journalists, could stop puzzling: The globetrotting, outspoken rebel *was* plying his trade anew in General Rene Barrientos's Bolivia.

In his "Manifesto," Ché spoke of his guerillas as the "National Liberation Army of the Bolivian People." "Overseers, generals, and Yankee imperialists," he wrote, "your claws and your jaws are red with the blood of the Bolivian people, and today your final hour has tolled. . . . The fight has begun and will not end until the day the people governs itself and foreign dominion has been wiped out. . . . Long live the guerillas!"

Ché's guerilla band was six months old in May 1966. His platoon occupied the villages of Caraguatarenda and Ipitacita, seizing several trucks and driving off toward an army stronghold at the Rio Grande. Victories, however, had not eliminated the guerillas' basic problems: Maps still misled, picturing roads and towns that did not exist; food was so scarce that the men were forced to eat a smelly, decaying coyote. Under a sun hot enough to crack stones, there were three more desertions—and Joaquín's platoon was lost again.

Ché had left the second platoon in the hamlet of Bella Vista, ordering Joaquín to make a temporary "demonstration." In retrospect he admitted that he'd only given the demonstration order so that the sickest guerillas would stay with Joaquín and not slow the first platoon's pace.

86

Yet separating from Joaquín was the major blunder of the guerilla campaign. Both platoons would search for each other in a wide, almost impenetrable area south of the Rio Grande. Without Joaquín's men, Ché would be divested of two thirds of his fast-tiring guerilla force.

By June army units had blocked an exit route from the Ñancahuazú River, causing Ché to hunt for Joaquín by crossing the mountains—an overwhelmingly difficult task. The trucks taken in Ipitacita were out of water, running only an extra day after Ché asked the men to urinate into the water tanks. In a mid-month skirmish, army blood-hounds were shot, but the guerillas lost Rolando, a man Ché described as a "pillar" of the group. Another death occurred on June 26, bullets flying back and forth near the town of Florida. Tuma was shot in the stomach, his intestines and liver destroyed. Ché operated on him, sterilizing a knife by fire, but Tuma died during the operation. "With his death," Ché wrote, "I lost an irreplaceable, truly loyal comrade of many years standing. . . . I miss him."

Ché's asthma gravely worsened in Bolivia's torrid summer. Those around him could see that his every breath was an agonizing battle. But Pombo and Braulio, keeping their own diaries, said that whenever guerilla life was "too much," Ché was an example of unflagging courage. On June 21, wheezing too hard to even walk, Ché wrote in his notebook, "For the first time in this war I was mounted on a mule." On July 3, with hardly any medicine left, he said simply, "My asthma continues making war."

It was the lack of Ché's medicine that led the guerillas into their most memorable Bolivian coup. Samaipata, a town on the Cochabamba–Santa Cruz highway, had no imperialist oil refinery to sabotage, but it had drugs and food. Ché seized a truck on the highway, abandoning its owner and driving with Ricardo, Coco, Urbano, Aniceto, Julio, and Chino into Samaipata. He jumped from the truck near a locked army post and held his gun on the post's chief and on two policemen stationed outside. "Give word to open the post!" he ordered the men. "And if you value your lives, get into the truck!"

The three men hesitated but jumped and jerked as Ché fired a volley of bullets at their feet. The post's chief shouted to a sentry behind a wall to open the gate. Then, with his policemen, he crawled shamefacedly into the rear of the truck while Samaipata's townspeople gaped from stores and cottages. Ché and his men corralled all of the post's soldiers into the main square. When one man resisted, he was immediately shot. The others stood awkwardly together.

Ché sent Chino into the stores to gather medicines and bandages. Ricardo and Urbano marched into a dozen or more cottages to search for food. Following his own rule, however, Ché would not allow any harm to the prisoners. "No violence without reason," he said. Prisoners would be stripped naked, taken to the woods, and released. The townspeople were as shocked at this leniency as they were when Ché, whom they slowly recognized from photos they'd seen, paid for food and pharmacy goods. Silent during the ten-hour occupation of Samaipata, the townspeople dashed, afterward, to surrounding villages, chattering of army surrender.

88

Bulletins and articles reporting the guerilla attack on Samaipata appeared in July's local and foreign newspapers. Was Samaipata, asked an editorial, a clear sign of army ineptitude in Bolivia? Was Ché Guevara, who might well be leading the guerilla pack, winning his newest anti-imperialist war?

Demoralized over the guerilla encroachment, Barrientos's officials—their regime tottering—met in near panic in the ornate government palace in La Paz. They were represented by a General Alfredo Ovando, who released a statement to the clamoring press. "I wish to announce," said General Ovando, "that the man commanding the guerillas *is* the famous Guevara. This may give an idea of the real significance of Ñancahuazú."

Ché, trying to breathe in the forests outside Samaipata, Bolivia, was back in the daily headlines. Even in the dense and enveloping cover of the Ñancahuazú Valley, he would be back in full view.

10

Although Ché had made the United States the brunt of his *imperialismo* ire, he was a hero there to certain student groups and liberal factions. To the liberals he was a champion of the have-nots. To the students, grappling in adolescence with their own "authority figures," he was the rebel against authority, a modern Robin Hood of the forests who assaulted the rich to reward the poor. Dozens of U.S. college dorm rooms of the late 1960s displayed posters of Ché while a Spanish song, composed by one of his guerillas, was translated into English:

Ernesto Guevara comes down from the hills to the city.
Now the guerilla fighters have a leader to follow.
Now he has passed through the mountains and already
*   can be seen in the woods,*
For Ernesto Guevara, fighting, lives and goes on. . . .

As Ché kept fighting, however, Bolivia's army finally turned the tide in its favor. Aided by U.S. Ranger troops, the army ambushed Ché's platoon on July 20, 1967, at the Morocos River. The guerillas dived into brush, escaping injury, but they lost weapons and walkie-talkies at the river. That night a peasant on a mule announced that soldiers had attacked Bolivian tin miners holding demonstrations against the government. "So Bolivia's troops have learned to shoot," Ché told his men. "We've shocked them into shape."

The army's skills increased during the month of August. Military training of soldiers by eleven U.S. specialists from Vietnam dealt Ché, on September 2, a devastating blow. Camped with his men on a cow path, he was turning the station knob on a radio from Samaipata when he heard the Voice of America broadcast. Ten guerillas, said the broadcast, had been killed by the army near Camiri, Bolivia. Other guerillas, taken prisoner, had identified the platoon leader, Joaquín, as one of the dead. The rebel movement's commander, Ché Guevara, was still at large.

On the cow path shadows merged and lengthened. Ché's mind bargained with what he had heard. He snapped the volume knob to its off position. *Propaganda,* he told himself. *Scare tactics from General Barrientos. Joaquín and the other guerillas couldn't be dead. Why, even at that moment they might be camped in the valley.*

Ché would go on denying the certainty of having lost eighteen guerilla fighters. Further radio reports of the scene at the water-crossed jungle area, Vado del Yeso, described the river bubbling red with the blood of guerillas

From a jungle outpost Ché poses with a rifle. Photos such as these, released by Fidel Castro, showed the world that Ché Guevara was always "where he will be most useful to the revolution." *AP/Wide World Photos.*

shot as they tried to swim from bank to bank. Ché condemned the broadcasts for lacking a "ring of truth." After all, he wrote in his diary on September 11, the radio had reported General Barrientos's declaring that Ché "had been dead for some time," only to quote, hours later, the General's "offering fifty thousand Bolivian pesos for information leading to his capture dead or alive"!

Joaquín *was* dead, however, as were ten and then eight more of the hapless second platoon. The actual "ring of truth" was that Ché's Bolivian Revolution was reduced to a mere twenty-one men. He had leaped into Bolivia to widen his "people's cause," to act out his extravagant ideas for creating social change. His book on guerilla warfare was the most popular military treatise in Latin America, but suddenly he was no longer winning his Bolivian war.

For Ché, Bolivia was not Cuba. Samaipata was not Santa Clara. He had ignited, with Fidel Castro, the revolutionary fervor of the discontented Cuban populace. But in Bolivia, though groups of tin miners had taken a cue from the *rebeldes'* 1957 mountain camps, declaring "free territories" at the mines, the frustrated tin miners and the isolated guerillas never increased their strengths by physically joining forces.

As for Bolivia's peasants, the most astounding fact of Ché's campaign in the Ñancahuazú Valley was that not a single peasant ever took up arms to fight with him. Poor, hungry, and oppressed, the Indian peasants saw the Barrientos government as a stern but dependable father. To defy the government, to fight for rights, was to ask for the

93

kind of trouble Ché always sought. Like the man with no legs who had spit on a young Ernesto Guevara in Alta Gracia, Argentina, the peasants accepted their lot.

As the 1967 summer spiraled downward, Ché and his men wandered through the mountain province of Vallegrande. The land was dry and craggy, with few animals or crops living on it. The mule that had carried Ché on his sickest days had to be butchered and cooked, and several army attacks took a quick, mordant toll. Coco Peredo, Miguel, and Julio were killed; Pacho suffered a "superficial wound through his buttocks and the skin of his testicles." Knapsacks of medication were grabbed by the army, and tiny as the guerilla band was, Ché sent five men to retrieve drugs stored in the second base camp.

Illness had been throttling most of the guerillas. Fainting spells were common among the "machete crew," and each day the men experienced violent diarrhea. Along with spasms of coughing and wheezing, of blood spit from his battered lungs, Ché diagnosed himself as "having a liver condition." He must have realized, as the army grew bolder, that his revolution was floundering. In eleven months he had failed to win the hearts of Bolivia's peasants. No matter how deeply he'd shaken the confidence of the Barrientos regime, he was not sustaining successes. He might have led his remaining men to safety over the northern borders to Brazil, but he did not. He was in mortal conflict with his afflictions, and he defied them even as he courted his fate. If he worried about his family or wondered why Fidel hadn't sent a rescue team to him, why Fidel had perhaps abandoned him, he didn't say. He was thirty-nine years old, close to what he'd called the "dead dreams of middle age." He had made his bed of continual unrest; he would live in it even if he choked himself to death.

In the first week of October General Barrientos offered amnesty to guerillas who voluntarily surrendered. The army, closing in on Ché and his men, blocked the north end of the Cochabamba–Santa Cruz highway, the south route at the Rio Grande, and the eastern pass at the Yacuiba–Santa Cruz railway. Still Ché did not seek escape. He hoped for some reinforcements from La Paz. When he was informed that a U.S.-trained, six-hundred-fifty-man army unit was in the nearby town of La Higuera, he shrugged. Yes, he had detailed the peril of encirclement by the army, but his guerillas were too sick to break any trap. Dividing the men into four groups, he hid them in the Yuro Ravine during the day. At night the groups reunited to plan an ambush outside La Higuera. Ravenous birds circled above them, drawn by their sores, sweat, and excrement. Washing clean at an open river, however, had become too dangerous for the men to attempt.

On October 7 Ché led his sixteen starving guerillas out of the Yuro Ravine to find food. Wheezing in a shrill, tinny sound, he leaned sharply to his left side to lessen the pain in his liver. He was fifteen pounds under his normal weight, his face chiseled and pale. If he had not been wearing his soiled uniform but had been outfitted in frock coat and collar, he would have looked the part of a fervent-eyed priest fused to his inward visions.

A mile from the ravine, footprints clearly imprinting across a potato field, the guerillas discovered an old peasant woman tending goats. Gray haired and stooped, the

95

woman barely raised her head as the men approached her. "We won't disturb you," Ché said. "We are here to help Bolivia's peasants. Times are difficult for us. Is the army nearby? Have you noticed soldiers?"

The woman, wiping her hands on an apron, kept her head lowered toward her chest. "No soldiers," she said. "Nothing. The army has gone."

Ché and Urbano glanced at each other, eyebrows raised. *"Gone?"* Ché said. "Well, that's . . . good. If soldiers happen to return, please don't say you've seen us."

"No, no," the woman mumbled. "Nothing."

Ché did not move forward toward the thistle-filled brush. The October sun cast an orange haze on the peasant woman's face, lighting the creases of her cheeks. He knew she was lying to him. The army had not withdrawn. That was why the woman would not raise her head, why she had mumbled.

The goats listlessly pawed at the earth as Ché watched the grim set of the peasant woman's mouth. He was totally convinced that she would soon show the army the guerillas' footprints in the field. She would divulge the exact number of his ill and encumbered men. It was not really surprising, he told himself—not at all. Time, breath, and renewal were too scant now, in the dark hollows of his mission's close, to avoid a final visit of the old hag and assassin called death.

On the night of October 8 Ché gathered his guerillas in Quelbrado del Yuro, a canyon. Chino no longer saw well enough to walk at night, and Ché had ordered a stop at

96

two A.M. Ditches in the canyon brimmed with foul water, but exhausted and thirsty, the men had thrust their faces into the largest ditch to slurp up mouthfuls of liquid. Afterward, rolling onto stomachs and backs, they had fallen asleep.

In the morning Ché awakened first. He stared up at the canyon's high, tree-studded rim, then flung himself diagonally behind a scraggly bush. "Get up!" he thundered at his men. "The army has surrounded us on the canyon top!"

Bolivian soldiers were peering down toward the distant specks of men who appeared to be their prey. Scattering the guerillas into patches of foliage, Ché tightened his grip on his rifle. A pulsing began at his temples; otherwise he was calm. Hadn't every second of his past days been directed toward this moment, this eventual reckoning? What else to expect?

At one thirty P.M., their ranks growing, the Eighth Division of U.S. Army Rangers initiated gunfire. The guerillas shot back in what would be a two-hour exchange of bullets. Sliding partway down the canyon walls, twenty or so soldiers slowly encircled their targets. Birds cawed piercingly, the wounded on both sides moaning beneath them. The wide slash of canyon mouth was gray under a cloudy sky, backdrop to the final October minuet. Three million dollars had been spent by the Barrientos government to teach its army how to lead the cornering dance against Ché Guevara's guerillas.

Just before three P.M., Ché was shot in the leg. Bullets shredded his skin below the knee, slamming into his tibia bone. The guerilla nicknamed Willy half dragged, half carried Ché up the canyon. Reaching the top in twenty-five minutes, he propped his wounded and gasping commander under a tree. Blood poured down the olive green of Ché's pant leg, but he gave orders to Willy to relay to the men. "They must split into their groups of four," Ché said. "One group will cover another with rifle fire. Tell them to climb to flat land. It's safer."

As Willy reluctantly turned to descend, a bullet struck him in the head. Wordlessly he crumpled down the canyon, a scarecrowlike figure in jacket and baggy pants. Four soldiers lunged out of a thicket, rifles cocked and aimed at Ché. "Don't shoot!" Ché said. "I am Ché Guevara, worth more to you alive than dead."

The soldiers, ecstatic over their prize capture after months of futile searching, tugged a bleeding Ché into the rear of a canvas-backed truck. Two more soldiers scrambled a quarter of the way down the canyon to tear Aniceto out of a tree. They hauled their second prisoner to the canyon top, throwing him, kicking and swearing, into the truck. Moments later Ché felt the grinding of wheels as the truck moved away. Willy was dead, his head blown apart; the other guerillas, Ché's old friend Urbano among them, waited in the canyon like sitting ducks.

Two miles to the north, in La Higuera, Ché and Aniceto were pushed from the truck into a two-room schoolhouse. Their pockets were emptied, their boots yanked off to be kept as souvenirs. "I had hoped to die with my boots *on*," Ché said wryly to one of the soldiers.

"Forget hopes, guerilla man," the soldier answered.

Taking off his shirt, Ché tied it around his leg to slow the streaming of blood. The schoolroom was empty of furniture, even of any ink to remind him of the glossy potion he'd swallowed in school as a child, and he sat on the dirt floor, leaning against a wall. Two soldiers put Aniceto in the next room, three remaining to guard the door. By nightfall Ché's ravaged leg was throbbing. He could see, in the moonlight through the window, a chunk of bone gleaming whitely from a jagged hole near his ankle. He had no instruments for extracting bullets. *No gun,* he thought, *no scalpel, no adrenaline inhaler.* No possibility for writing last letters to Aleida, Hilda, and the children; to Fidel or to his father, brothers, and sisters; to his friend Alberto Granados. He knew he could have been a better husband and father, but the idea of family had become so remote to him—his marriage a sacrifice to the ever-beguiling revolution.

At dawn on October 9 Colonel Zenteno of the Bolivian Army, accompanied by two sergeants, eight soldiers, and six CIA agents, arrived at the La Higuera schoolhouse. Ché's comments to them would be carried to the waiting journalists and printed repeatedly in newspapers. Ché talked of the 1962 blockade of Cuba as having led to a rising anti-American sentiment in Latin America. He referred to Cuba's growth as a world power and to its challenge to capitalist-imperialist philosophy in North America. Regarding Bolivia, he said, he was disappointed in the peasants. The Indian population had let a greed-oriented, American-backed military regime grind them into pulp as useless as their trance-making coca leaves.

99

Colonel Zenteno motioned one of his sergeants, a man named Mario Terán, out of the room. "You have crazy, Marxist ideas," the colonel told Ché. "If Bolivia put you on trial for war crimes, the publicity would do you too much good."

Death, Ché was sure, was just a few labored breaths away. He was worth more, it seemed, *dead* than alive. A shot burst its sound through the schoolhouse, and he thought the bullet had penetrated his body. He expected to see blood and to feel pain somewhere other than in his shattered leg, but he soon realized that the shot had come from the next room. The anguished cry he heard must have been uttered by Aniceto.

Footsteps brought Sergeant Terán back into Ché's sight. Colonel Zenteno stood squarely by the window, flanked by his ten personnel and by the six CIA agents. "Well, Guevara," said Sergeant Terán, his gun cocked and shining in his hand, "what do you think on this bright October morning?"

Sitting again against the wall, Ché smiled at the sergeant. "I think," he said, digging only his fingernails into the dirt floor, keeping the rest of himself perfectly immobile, "that we cannot be certain of having something to live for unless we're willing to die for it."

The two bullets answered him, one ripping into his throat after he spoke, the other blasting into the left side of his chest. His mouth opened, perhaps to expel one last unsettling word or to suck in a last asthma-hammered breath. In several seconds, however, completing the old stories of nearly fatal attacks of breathlessness, of nearly

100

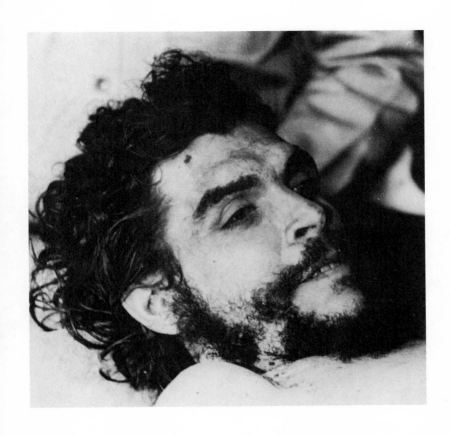

Ché, dead for over a day, is carried from a helicopter on a canvas litter into a waiting horde of newspapermen and journalists in Vallegrande, Bolivia. *AP/Wide World Photos.*

fatal sieges of bullets, he moved freely and unflinchingly into death.

It was eight months before Ché's fortieth birthday. He would be pictured on that October morning as serene of face—his feet, divested of their boots, clean and amazingly dustless. "He looked," said one of the men in the La Higuera schoolhouse, "still alive and, in a strange manner, acutely aware of us. Ché Guevara and his revolution were somehow still with us."

AFTERMATH

Did Ché remain "alive"? Does he live on within the sagas of stalwart adventurers, of rebellious dreamers who see real danger in the strictures of bureaucracy and authority? Ché's death triggered a host of opposing tales. He was, claimed Colonel Zenteno of Bolivia, justifiably killed in battle. *No,* said circulating rumors: Ché was executed to cut short his influence or any sympathy for him. He sustained, said the Associated Press, only leg and throat wounds—though his fingers were later chopped off to prove, through his fingerprints, that he'd truly died. *No,* said an autopsy report from a Dr. José Caso: death-causing wounds occurred in Ché's heart and lungs.

And his burial? Ché was already "buried in the town of Vallegrande," announced Bolivia's General Ovando on

October 11, 1967. The next day, hounded by journalists wanting to see the grave, General Ovando changed his story. "The armed forces," said the General, "have cremated Ché Guevara."

The world press, along with hundreds of thousands of world citizens, kept Ché "alive." In Cuba, Fidel Castro had a mammoth portrait of his famous comandante mounted in the vast Plaza de la Revolución. Spotlights played over the portrait while Fidel, his friend no longer a political liability, presented an address about Ché's inspiring call for the "New Man." Cuban schools, hospitals, plazas, and streets were renamed for Ché; Cuban Communist poet Nicolás Guillén composed a classical ode to him. In Argentina, land of Ché's birth, demonstrating students who refused to believe reports of Ché's death demanded his "release from a Bolivian prison," while Padre Hernán Benítez, confessor to Argentine political leaders, commented: "Just as the medieval Spaniards always believed El Cid Campeador had not died, so is it possible that in future years the soldiers of the third world will feel the presence of Ché in the ardor of guerilla struggle."

In Italy and West Germany students—shouting *"Ché lives!"*—planted bombs in the Bolivian Embassy. In France leftist artists, writers, and teachers celebrated a "Ché Guevara week." Photos of Ché were sold on European streets and set up in homes, apartments, and grottos beside burning candles and Bibles. The Uruguayan priest Juan Zaffaroni called Ché "the revolutionary I idolize"; the *Monthly Review*, a liberal United States journal, went so far as to print a poem labeling him "the rebel Christ." Only in Russia were the obituaries brief; everywhere else even Ché's multitude of detractors could not stop talking of him.

In the years since his death, Ché has become a provocative symbol of the quintessential guerilla fighter, the rash and undaunted objector. Books have been published about him; his Bolivian notebooks were printed. In 1968, with Pombo, Urbano, and Benigno—the only guerillas to escape from the Yuro Ravine—Hilda wrote an article on her ex-husband and the Bolivian revolution, followed, in 1972, by her book *Ernesto: A Memoir of Ché Guevara.* "The unredeemed people are still here," Hilda wrote. "You [Ché] will always be present in our struggles."

Ché's children have remained in Cuba. His son is a doctor; all his children embrace his principles of revolution. Ché's father moved from Buenos Aires to Havana, where Fidel welcomed him into the fold. While Fidel in the 1980s continues as Prime Minister of Cuba, Latin America struggles on, a hotbed of conflicting politics. In Bolivia in 1985 Victor Paz Estenssoro, reelected president, inherited Latin America's poorest economy, the average annual pay being five hundred forty U.S. dollars. In Argentina the yearly inflation rate soared as high as 900 percent as military regimes and more democratic forms of government ebbed and flowed. Guerillas of the 1980s fight for their separate causes in Central America's Nicaragua and El Salvador, sharp reminders of Ché in their jungle battles against the political structures in their countries. And in Europe, Asia, Africa, and the United States,

105

though justice sometimes triumphs without Ché's brand of violent reform, the haves and the have-nots still lock horns in recurrent outcry.

On April 3, 1987, in the city of Santiago, Chile, thousands of antigovernment protestors stoned police, journalists, and priests in a park where Pope John Paul II came to celebrate a Mass urging national reconciliation. Amid the chaos of police reprisal—water cannons, tear gas, shotgun pellets—placards displaying a man's face were raised above the crowds by demonstrators. It was Ché's face on the placards—intense, confronting eyes piercing as blades. *"Ché Lives!"* were the familiar painted words on brightly colored banners.

Ché never sought reconciliation, as had the Pope and many other prudent and caring leaders in history. He favored violence over humanism in fighting for equality among people. He was a repository of anger and retaliation rather than of peace, his asthma partly a childhood voice of pain and protest. He could be tender and cruel, killing when he thought it necessary, acting mercifully when he chose, as ready with a gun as with a word. He had won in Cuba, lost in Bolivia, his mission basically commendable but his methods open to disavowal and condemnation.

Twenty years past his death Ché's image has been carried aloft by demonstrators who still see him as he had hoped to be seen—as a dissenter against repression of the masses, a voice of protest and of active combat in the name of the oppressed. Ché's own assumed name means, after all, "any fellow, anywhere." He chose the name "Ché"

106

on a fiery, battle-scarred street in Guatemala to make his statement about equality. The revolution became for Ché Ernesto Guevara the most enduring and defiant cause he could manage to breathe deeply into himself.

BIBLIOGRAPHY

The most important sources for this book were Ché's diaries. These are available in English and are worth reading:

Guevara, Ché. *Bolivian Diary, Ernesto "Ché" Guevara.* Translated by Carlos P. Hansen and Andrew Sinclair. London: Jonathan Cape, Ltd./ Lorimer, 1968.

Guevara, Ché. *The Complete Bolivian Diaries of Ché Guevara and Other Captured Documents.* Edited by Daniel James. New York: Stein & Day, Publishers, 1968.

Guevara, Ché. *Reminiscences of the Cuban Revolutionary War.* Translated by Victoria Ortiz. New York: Monthly Review Press, 1968.

Books by Ché's companions give a picture of what he was like in action. These include:

109

Gadea, Hilda. *Ernesto: A Memoir of Ché Guevara.* New York: Doubleday & Company, Inc., 1972.

Rojo, Ricardo. *My Friend Ché.* New York: The Dial Press, Inc., 1968.

Some accounts by outsiders that have valuable insights are:

Eden, Martin. *Ché: The Making of a Legend, Guerilla Hero of a Generation in Revolt.* New York: Universe Books, 1969.

Gonzales, Luis J. *The Great Rebel: Ché Guevara in Bolivia.* New York: Grove Press, Inc., 1969.

Harris, Richard. *Death of a Revolutionary: Ché Guevara's Last Mission.* New York: W. W. Norton & Company, Inc., 1970.

James, Daniel. *Ché Guevara.* New York: Stein & Day, Publishers, 1969.

A fascinating adult novel based on Ché is:

Cantor, Jay. *The Death of Ché Guevara.* New York: Alfred A. Knopf, 1983.

The following articles are useful for the serious student:

Blackburn, Robin. "Ten Years Without Ché." *New Statesman*, Vol. 94, Oct. 7, 1977, pp. 465–66.

"Death of a Dreamer." Anonymous. *Commonweal*, Vol. 103, Oct. 27, 1967.

Marchant, H.S. "Guevara, Man & Myth." *Encounter*, Vol. 31, Dec. 1968, pp. 56–61.

Martin, Delores Moyano. "A Memoir of the Young Guevara." *The New York Times Magazine*, Aug. 18, 1968, pp. 48–59.

Ray, Michelle. "The Execution of Ché by the CIA." *Ramparts*, Vol. 6, Mar. 1968, pp. 21–27.

AUTHOR'S NOTE

Ché tasted both triumph and defeat. The conflicts in his life, the deep hunger in his search to find his own destiny, and his struggle to bring dignity and equality to all human beings inspired me to study and then tell his life. His lengthy diaries, and the memoirs of his companions, provided a fine glimpse into his inner thoughts and responses. This book is a fictionalized biography: I have invented some of the scenes and dialogues, but it is also faithful to Ché as I came to know him.

Ché was an authentic rebel. He was provocative and defiant, never afraid to take a chance or to swim against the tide. Like many heroes, Ché's legend was born while he was still alive, and whenever we remember his courage and honor, his spirit lives on.

113